Quail Lakes & Coal

Energy for Wildlife ... And the World

DOUG OBERHELMAN

With Diane Oberhelman and Jeff Lampe

AuthorHouse™
1663 Liberty Drive
Bloomington, IN 47403
www.authorhouse.com
Phone: 1-800-839-8640

© 2013 Doug Oberhelman. All rights reserved.

No part of this book may be reproduced, stored in a retrieval system, or transmitted by any means without the written permission of the author.

Published by AuthorHouse 1/23/2013

ISBN: 978-1-4817-0999-6 (sc)
ISBN: 978-1-4817-0997-2 (hc)
ISBN: 978-1-4817-0998-9 (e)

Library of Congress Control Number: 2013901141

Any people depicted in stock imagery provided by Thinkstock are models, and such images are being used for illustrative purposes only. Certain stock imagery © Thinkstock.

This book is printed on acid-free paper.

Because of the dynamic nature of the Internet, any web addresses or links contained in this book may have changed since publication and may no longer be valid.

The views expressed in this work are solely those of the author and do not necessarily reflect the views of the publisher, and the publisher hereby disclaims any responsibility for them.

authorHOUSE®

*To my wife, my best friend in the whole world,
and my co-author Diane, I thank you.*

Contents

Foreword One ....Greg Boyce 7

Foreword Two ....Dale Hall 9

Foreword Three.........German Larrea 11

Preface...13

Map of Quail Lakes 17

Introduction..19

Chapter 1 ....*Settling the Land of Black Gold* 23

Chapter 2 ....*Illinois Mining Comes of Age* 47

Chapter 3 ....*Mining at Quail Lakes* 67

Chapter 4 ....*We Can Reclaim It*......................................85

Chapter 5 ....*The Wildlife Respond*s.............................105

Chapter 6 ....*From Wasteland to Wonderland*...............127

Chapter 7 ....*The Coal Solution* 141

End Notes and Bibliography 151

FOREWORD ONE

In *Quail Lakes & Coal — Energy for Wildlife ... And the World*, Doug Oberhelman powerfully chronicles the history of a remarkable place and the rise of one of the most successful — and little-known — U.S. public-private partnerships to benefit the environment and economy. Quail Lakes is a 1,200-acre example of the transformation of a landscape from wilderness to surface-mined land and "back to the wild."

Importantly, the deep clear lakes, prime farmland, and wildlife habitat at Quail Lakes are not unique. They can be found on former mined lands in every corner of the country. The U.S. coal-mining industry has embraced sustainable land use and pioneered the science of land restoration. Every day my company sends scientists and experts around the world to restore mined properties to meet the needs of communities and nations.

Too often debates about energy policies drift toward unsustainable mandates or punitive measures — at the expense of proven, affordable solutions. Oberhelman describes another model — an approach to empowering people and businesses to conserve through innovation and investment. He has long supported protecting wildlife in natural habitats, while taking into account the need for a strong economy driven by low-cost energy.

The story of Quail Lakes is proof that we can develop a vital and reliable domestic energy resource and achieve the parallel goal of environmental progress for ourselves and for future generations.

—GREG BOYCE
Chairman and CEO, Peabody Energy

FOREWORD TWO

My personal opinions have been formed by experiences that stem from two seemingly opposing catalysts: growing up in the coal-mine country of Harlan County, Kentucky, and an entire career with the U.S. Fish and Wildlife Service and Ducks Unlimited trying to conserve natural resources for future generations.

What I have learned is that in order to have people become conservation-minded, they must be able to make an adequate living and secure affordable energy to care for their families. Conservation becomes a luxury if your family is hungry. Coal is one of those sources of economy and energy, and the long-term solution rests in new technologies and new commitments to care for and restore the land to as near natural condition as possible once the energy has been extracted.

As Doug and Diane Oberhelman's story attests, new techniques allow habitat restoration once thought impossible to be the new reality. What the Oberhelmans have done on their Quail Lakes property in Illinois should be a case study in positive actions taken by responsible coal operators and landowners, and their story should be shared across this great nation wherever coal is being mined or plans are under way to extract this abundant source of jobs and energy. It proves success can occur when businesses and landowners are willing to work together for common good.

—H. DALE HALL
CEO, Ducks Unlimited Inc, and
Director, U.S. Fish and Wildlife Service (Retired)

FOREWORD THREE

At Grupo Mexico, we understand that sustainability is a challenge for us all. Generating value in our surroundings is the unquestionable vocation of our company. Every member of this big family contributes to this mission and we are also committed to managing our work responsibly.

Our U.S. affiliate ASARCO, with its team of experts in responsible management, has also contributed to the sustainability of mining with successful reclamation efforts at Midland Coal Company properties in Illinois.

We congratulate Doug Oberhelman, who has purchased some 1,200 acres of these reclaimed parcels from ASARCO over the past several years to restore and develop into a wildlife habitat treasure named Quail Lakes. The journey this land has taken surely affords a glimpse into civilization's productive and sustainable use of land – past, present, and future.

—GERMAN LARREA
Chairman and CEO, Grupo Mexico

PREFACE

Birds and wildlife have always fascinated me. Since I was a kid growing up in northern Illinois I've enjoyed watching wild animals and reading books about nature and conservation. One favorite is the *Smithsonian Birds of North America* by Fred Alsop. I turn to that reference often and appreciate the words within. But I never had aspirations to write a book. Actually, I'm not a very good writer. Even so, for the past few years I've had an idea for a book — not so much to write but to tell what I think is quite a story.

Like many landowners, my wife Diane and I are passionate about our property. In particular, we have a deep attachment to the 1,200-acre central Illinois farm we call Quail Lakes. Our attachment is so deep that we don't really take typical "vacations" like most families. When we do have free time, we almost always spend it at Quail Lakes. We don't have another vacation home. And I've all but abandoned my golf game. Quail Lakes is our place to relax and recharge.

It was during our visits to the property that the idea for this book grew. At first we set out to trace the path of Native Americans and settlers who walked the land before us, to learn more about mining and restoration on the property, and to tell about the abundant wild animals and birds we have encountered. We also believe that few pieces of property have had so many productive uses as this one.

Two things stood in the way of me writing this book. Since July 1, 2010, I've had my hands full serving as the Chairman and Chief Executive Officer of Caterpillar Inc., the company I've worked for since graduating from Millikin University in 1975. Then too there is the issue of actually writing. As I mentioned, composing paragraphs is not my greatest strength.

That's why I approached Jeff Lampe to help. I first met Jeff while he was working as outdoor columnist for the *Peoria Journal Star*. Diane and I enjoyed his writing and we kept in touch over the years, as we share similar passions for hunting, land conservation, and wildlife. We also share similar geography. Jeff and his family live in the wonderful town of Elmwood, just a few miles north of Quail Lakes. They moved there in part to be closer to surface mines — properties that offer some of the best hunting and fishing in Illinois. Hunting is a priority for Jeff and for me. In fact, the first time we met about this book was in a duck blind at The Rice Pond Preserve on the Illinois River. We've also had "meetings" during dove and goose hunts at Quail Lakes.

The book evolved over the course of those meetings. Telling the tale of Quail Lakes is still the focus, but in the process of writing this history, we came to see the book as more than a mere timeline of occupancy and land use of a 1,200-acre Illinois farm. For me, Quail Lakes is a timely example of the many benefits we can reap from the land when we work responsibly. I don't think there are many places on earth that have had so many and varied land uses. Yet if somebody drove out to visit they would never know Quail Lakes was once a surface mine with pits dug 75 feet into the earth.

That to me is the essence of this story.

I have no great expectations for this book from a sales standpoint, but to the extent *Quail Lakes & Coal* does sell, any proceeds we generate will go to Ducks Unlimited — an organization I admire and support. At the same time, I hope the book and the story of Quail Lakes might inspire others to pursue conservation on their land. And I'd like to think this story might be a small part of ongoing debates about coal mining and energy use in the United States.

There are also plenty of people to thank. Diane is atop my list because she is as passionate about hunting, fishing, and conservation as I am, and because she has been actively involved in our work at Quail Lakes. We enjoy many special moments at our farm with family and friends and with Diane's four children and their spouses: Allen, Alison, Kathleen (and husband Tyson Brill), and Maureen (and husband Chris Bennett). Allen deserves credit for coining the catchy name Quail Lakes for our property. I've also enjoyed good times with my nieces Candice Smith (and her husband Derek) and Dana Gustafson, and with Candice's children, Colin and Caden.

Many others deserve credit, as well.

Our neighbor Bill Atwood of Elmwood is a good friend who has done yeoman's work at Quail Lakes. He helps run the Caterpillar equipment we own and is always willing to help improve the property. It has also been fun watching Bill turn into a birdwatcher. When I first met him I'm not sure he knew a robin from a cardinal. Today he'll call me with news about which field the snow geese are using or any other wildlife he has seen.

I'd like to thank the Natural Resources Conservation Service, which helped design our terraces, dry dams, and wetlands. Credit for design work of those terraces also goes to the Peoria Soil and Water Conservation District and to Jerry Wyatt. Pheasants Forever helped with prairie plantings, as did brothers Ron and Ted Gilles, who visited Quail Lakes to provide insight into prairie restoration and helped open my eyes to what was possible. Nate Herman had great ideas for the fish we stocked and he and his crew have built angler-friendly docks. Sam Dilsaver has done a fine job managing Elmwood Farms LLC dairy, another neighbor with whom we work closely.

As far as the text for the book, many deserve a pat on the back. Mike Kepple offered insight from a lifetime in surface-mining country. So did John O'Reilly and Eric Schenck. Dickson Mounds archaeologist Alan Harn was a rock-solid source for Illinois history. Special thanks goes to Jim Grimm, Phil Christy, and Ken Miars for stories of the Elm Mine, to Richard Coon for his fond memories of a Marion monster shovel, and to Harold Jehle for input on the banking industry. Norm Emerick and Ken Russell drew on years of in-the-mine experience to discuss fish, fowl, and other animals. Bruce Howard of Elmwood provided wonderful pictures and historic accounts, as did Doug Whitney and the Elmwood Historical Society.

Jeff asked me to thank his wife, Monica, and their three sons — Henry, Victor, and Walter — for putting up with him while he immersed himself in this story at the expense of fishing trips into the surface mines. But Jeff's three boys and generations after them will enjoy the benefits of similar restoration efforts here and around the world. Jeff also credits his parents, Dave and Ruth Lampe, with instilling his love for language as well as nitpicking over this manuscript. And he thanks brother-in-law Tony Vandercar for his graphic art skills.

Thanks goes to my hunting and fishing buddies at Quail Lakes and The Rice Pond: to Allen Cullinan, Dick and Mike Laukitis, Jerry Foley, Rex Linder, Chris Curfman, Don Welch, and so many others.

Having thanked all of those people, I am sure there are some that I

Doug Oberhelman

have forgotten to recognize. For that I am truly sorry. I also want to make it clear that I am responsible for any omissions or mistakes in this book. This is a personal endeavor by Diane and me. Neither Caterpillar nor Ducks Unlimited is responsible for the content of this book. And I regret if any information contained within these pages is incorrect or is not properly attributed. We have done our best to present an interesting, factual history of what I consider to be a fascinating piece of property.

—Doug Oberhelman
January, 2013

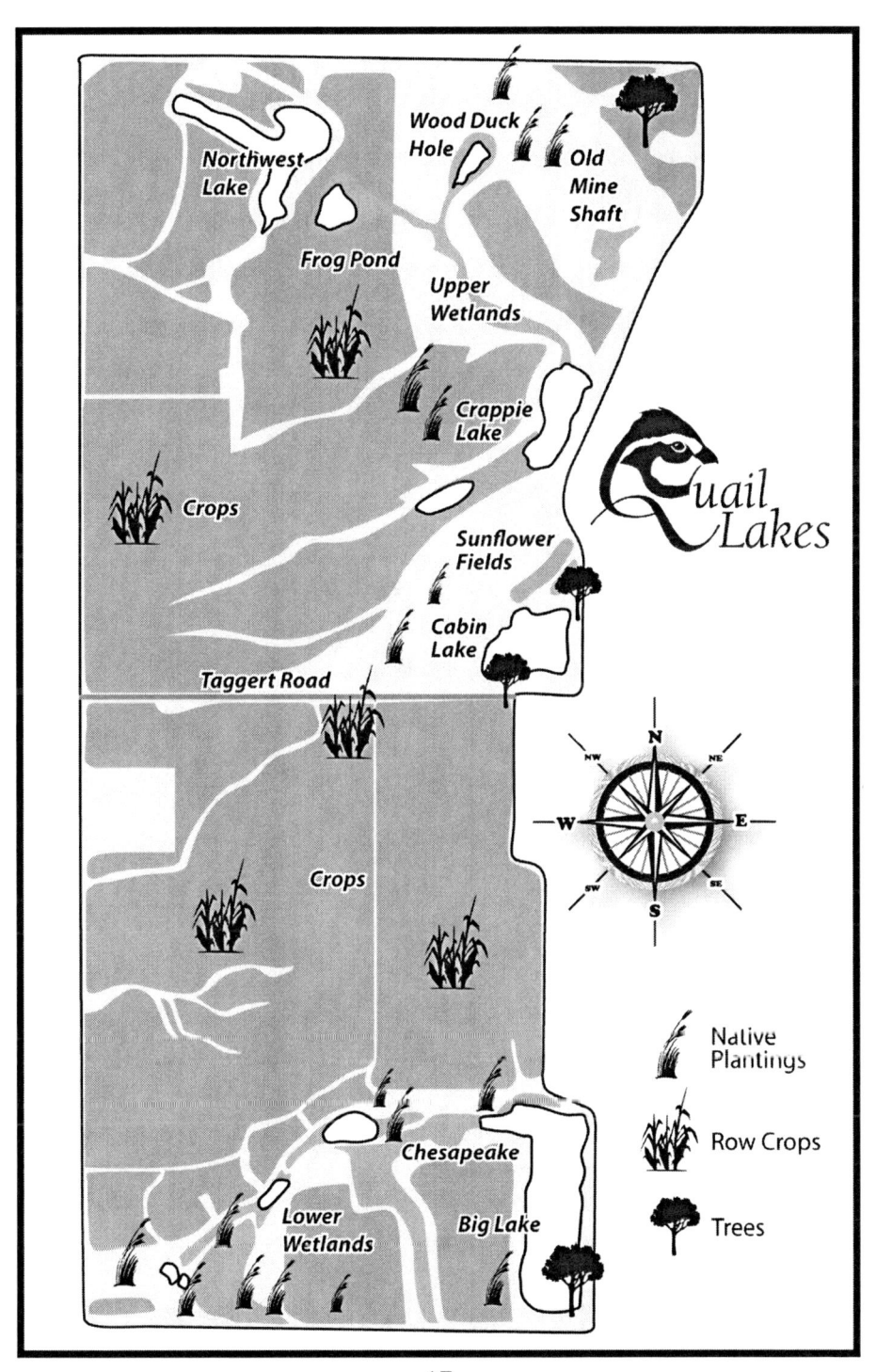

Quail Lakes & Coal

Doug Oberhelman

Quail Lakes & Coal

INTRODUCTION

Grass graced the Illinois landscape long before the stripping shovel, dragline or bucket-wheel excavator started scooping ... thousands of years before Cat D8 bulldozers began moving black dirt to uncover black coal. These were not the imported, cool-season grass species we are accustomed to seeing around homes or on baseball fields, but rather tall, native prairie grasses. Now big bluestem and other prairie plants have returned to the 1,200-acre Quail Lakes property my wife Diane and I own in central Illinois — a flowing reminder of the healing power of time ... and of mankind. It makes me smile to think that a wild land settled by a fascinating man named Avery Dalton is going wild again even after being intensively mined for coal.

Our property is part of an evolving history of land use. All inhabitants of earth leave an imprint relative to the technology available to them. That's as true of Native Americans 5,000 years ago who used stone hoes to dig burial mounds as it is of mining companies today who uncover coal with Bucyrus draglines and loaders made by Caterpillar.

Yes, the scale is different today. So is the population. Needs are greater because there are so many more people with so many more demands. That has become clear to me during my career with Caterpillar. I'm biased, but proud to say the company makes the world's finest earthmoving and mining equipment, as well as many other products that help make for a better world. Caterpillar's products make land use easier for an ever-growing world population. The balance we seek is to mitigate disturbance and to make land use sustainable. This story offers one example of what is possible.

Since the generally accepted birth of surface mining in the 1860s in Vermilion County, Illinois, "strip mining" has had a checkered history. While the United States has always — and will always — need affordable sources of energy, many early attempts at surface mining for coal left the land scarred. Gob piles of shale, clay, and rocky soil stand as a testament to these first mines, as do gashes in the ground lined by rocky, saw-tooth hills. "Like Hell with the fires put out," is how one observer described an abandoned surface mine where water ran red and spoil banks were devoid of vegetation or wildlife.

No question, the picture was not always pretty in the early days of the United States. Such was the history of our developing nation. Settlers found an often-hostile land filled with strange prairie plants, hordes of insects, and Native Americans who were not always excited by the arrival of so many new visitors. No wonder settlers were more concerned with surviving than with preserving the environment.

So like the Native Americans before them, they used the land. The coal that Avery Dalton mined after arriving in Peoria County in 1837 helped heat his home and the homes of many other neighbors. The same would be true throughout the U.S. as industrialization spread. Coal powered the country's growth. First came survival. Then profit. Only later were people afforded the relative luxury of time and the relative affluence to protect and to sustain the environment.

You can trace that change in the very laws that govern mining reclamation. The surface mining industry went from wide-open to closely regulated, due mostly to the 1977 Surface Mining Control and Reclamation Act. The property we call Quail Lakes is a prime example of that federal reclamation law in practice. From 1976 to 1984, Quail Lakes was surface mined by Midland Coal Company, which sent the coal to central Wisconsin to generate electricity. Once mining stopped, Midland restored the rolling complex of wetlands, lakes, agricultural fields, and grassy plantings. The dramatic reshaping was required by federal law but has also been supplemented by a conservation ethic.

Today, tillable ground yields corn, alfalfa, and wheat, sometimes reaching 90 percent of pre-mining yields. Crops are grown in a symbiotic relationship with a nearby dairy. Waste from the dairy herd is added to the ground, providing much-needed nutrients that boost yields. Grains and hay raised on the farm are fed to the dairy herd. I like to think about babies in St. Louis and in Peoria, Illinois, drinking milk from cows that feed off our land.

Quail Lakes feeds more than cows, though. Alongside our tillable ground you will find abundant wildlife habitat. Of Quail Lakes' 1,200 acres, more than 400 are in water, wetlands or native plantings. Big bluestem, the towering grass that made settlers quake, is back on the landscape. So are wildflowers of all sorts, providing an ever-changing display of color from spring through fall.

There's more water on the Quail Lakes landscape, as well. Deep, clear final-cut lakes are a byproduct of surface mining that offer wonderful wildlife habitat. Diane and I have also added shallow, seasonal wetlands. Once common in Illinois, these ephemeral shallow wetlands are increasingly rare as water is hastily drawn off the land. By adding grass and wetlands, we have attracted animals of all sorts. Bobwhite quail. Pheasants. Wild turkeys. Bald eagles. Whitetail deer. Salamanders. Snakes. Coyotes. Foxes. Frogs. Herons.

Along with these more common Illinois creatures have come state-endangered species like the northern harrier hawk and the short-eared owl. We've seen swans and loons and geese and ducks of all sorts. Since both Diane and I are passionate waterfowlers and long-time members of Ducks Unlimited, witnessing the spring and fall migration of waterfowl through our property is always gratifying and sometimes awe-inspiring. Several of our fields have been pure white in February and March as snow geese return north to their breeding grounds on the tundra.

Fish abound in the lakes where loaders carved out tons of bituminous coal. One lake is even home to rainbow trout, a species that needs cool water to survive a sizzling Illinois summer. Fortunately for the trout, final-cut lakes provide exactly that sort of habitat — deep and clear water that is cool enough to keep these colorful fish thriving through 90- and even 100-degree days of July and August.

Quail Lakes stands in stark contrast to some nearby surface mines. Due west of our property are thousands of acres that were mined in the 1960s. On these older sites you will find very little tillable ground and the evidence of mining is clear in high-sided, saw-toothed banks, exposed shale, and limited contouring of the land. Those older mine areas are altered forever. Quail Lakes is very different. Ours is a property that went from grassland to farmland to coal mine and now has gone back to farmland and grassland. What started wild in the early 1800s before settlement is returning to the wild — while still generating income.

The story of Quail Lakes is a remarkable odyssey that has been, and can be, repeated all over Illinois and across the United States. And it's one we need to see more often in the years to come. Like it or not, the inconvenient truth is that coal is part of the solution for America's en-

Doug Oberhelman

ergy puzzle. The U.S. is rightly called the Saudi Arabia of coal thanks to our abundant reserves. Relative to other energy sources coal is cheap to mine and to utilize.

Advancements in heavy equipment by Caterpillar and others make mining coal easier and more efficient. New technologies offer the real possibility that we can operate clean coal-fired plants — even with high-sulfur coal like that found in Illinois — with much less impact on the environment and atmosphere. Coal has been critical to our growth as a nation and with some technological innovation can be just as important to our continued growth.

Despite widespread negative press about surface mining, the story of Quail Lakes points to something very different. Our property provided the energy to light homes and businesses in Wisconsin while also providing crops to feed generations of farmers and livestock. Much of our land is still producing crops. But not all of it. On the acres left to grass and water, wildlife flocks. Quail Lakes also offers wonderful opportunities for recreation — for fishing, hunting, hiking, camping, swimming, wildlife watching, stargazing, and anything else you might dream of doing in a place where wild animals roam and stars shine bright.

I see Quail Lakes as a microcosm for the realistic and responsible use of land that is entirely possible today. In these pages we hope to plot a historic blueprint of an efficient, profitable, and self-sustainable example of what modern surface mining can provide. Jobs. Energy. Food. Habitat. Fun.

CHAPTER ONE
SETTLING THE LAND OF BLACK GOLD

When Avery Dalton walked into Elmwood Township in 1837, he could not have known how much black gold lay hidden below the gently rolling Illinois grasslands. Though Dalton would live to the ripe old age of 104, he had no way of knowing the land he settled in Peoria County and called Lost Prairie would someday light houses in Wisconsin, produce 200 bushels of corn per acre, attract thousands of geese each winter, and put milk in cereal bowls in Peoria and St. Louis.

Still Dalton believed there was potential when he came west to Illinois. Like so many settlers in the era of Manifest Destiny he arrived with thoughts of a better life. That promise had a magnetic attraction in the 1800s — a time when life was often hard and folks believed there had to be a better living somewhere. Many built a better life. Some perished. Some kept moving, never finding what they were searching for. Dalton was one of the lucky settlers. He came west and found a home and prosperity on the very same property — Section 19 of Elmwood Township — that my wife Diane and I call Quail Lakes.

Avery Dalton celebrates his 104th birthday in this photograph taken on Dec. 20, 1912. Photo courtesy of Bruce Howard.

Doug Oberhelman

The landscape that greeted Dalton in western Peoria County was mostly tallgrass prairie with stands of oak-hickory timber snaking along creeks and streams, including a tree-lined tributary of Kickapoo Creek that runs through the northeast corner of Section 19. Prairie chickens were likely common, as were a variety of other grassland birds whose songs we seldom hear today. Ducks and geese of all sorts nested or migrated along the Illinois River — though it is unlikely they lingered at Quail Lakes, since there was very little water on the property in the 1800s.

Dalton also saw and hunted wild turkeys, deer, squirrels, and raccoons — the Big Four of forest wildlife at the time of settlement. He may have encountered an occasional elk or bison wandering past. We know for certain Avery Dalton spent time with Native Americans, as he was said to be fluent in several native tongues and spoke often of dealings with Potawatomi tribe members, some of whom resided near Elmwood in what was then called Kickapoo Grove.

Quail Lakes, or Lost Prairie as the Daltons called it, obviously treated the family well. Once they arrived in 1837, Avery and his wife Delilah (or Delila in some historic records) stayed put for 63 years. After years of wandering as a young man, Avery Dalton seemed happy to find a home. "We moved but once in our lives," Dalton told a newspaper reporter around his 100th birthday, "moved to Lost Prairie and stayed there. Here we reared nine children. We both worked hard. We always had deer in our yard, and at night I heard the wild turkeys gobble. I used to shoot them from my back door. We always had venison."

Reading that made me shake my head at the similarities to my own life. Diane and I still walk out the back door of our cabin at Quail Lakes and hunt. And she is as sure a shot as anyone I've ever hunted with, even after switching from shooting right-handed to shooting left-handed due to a surgery a few years ago. Avery Dalton would have been proud of her. In the fall we can just walk out, go to one of our hunting pits or blinds, and shoot a duck or goose. We can fish right off the dock. Many game and fish species are as plentiful today as they were when Avery was putting food on the table in the 1800s. Like the Daltons, we always have a gun around and we're always ready to harvest something ... and to eat it later.

Dalton carved a living from the land — first as a farmer who raised

Members of the Dalton family cut and haul logs in the 1800s, a common job for settlers. Photo courtesy of Bruce Howard.

crops and livestock, later as a coal miner. He and his sons changed the landscape dramatically, plowing under much of the big bluestem prairie that had dominated the area. They cut trees to build fences and to provide fuel to keep warm in winter. They planted corn, oats, hay, and potatoes. They hunted wild game and fished the creeks.

Eventually they tunneled under the prairie to mine coal that warmed their homes and helped fuel the industry of Elmwood, the nearest town. But the Daltons were not the first to use the land. Not by a long shot. There's a perception that settlers ruined what had been a prosaic, perfect, unaltered landscape. That's not true. No question settlers made dramatic changes — and faster than any previous inhabitants. That was true in part because their numbers were so great, as noted by Taoyateduta, a Dakota chief who was quoted by Hanford Lennox Gordon as saying: "The white men are like the locusts when they fly so thick that the whole sky is a snowstorm. … Count your fingers all day long and white men with guns in their hands will come faster than you can count."

But people have always left a mark on the land — dating back to the earliest inhabitants of Illinois. The arrival of settlers was just one part of a 12,000-year timeline of habitation. Like the settlers, native inhabitants of Illinois also made their mark on the landscape. "Every one of them changed the land in some way," said Alan Harn, who has studied native populations for more than 50 years as an assistant curator of anthropology at Dickson Mounds Museum near Lewistown, Illinois. "Early on it was very minimal. But as populations began to consolidate and become permanent, they dug big holes in the ground for storage and houses and to bury their dead. They began to make an impact."

Those native inhabitants did not have Cat D9 tractors or huge Bucyrus-Erie draglines, just stone hoes and primitive tools. Still they left a footprint, sometimes larger than you might expect.

Pinning down precise residents of Quail Lakes in the earliest days is nearly impossible. The site has never been surveyed by archaeologists and never will be, since surface mining altered any record of past inhabitants. Thanks to research by historians at the Illinois State Museum and Dickson Mounds Museum, we can offer a rough sketch of likely inhabitants. Thanks to the historians we know that Paleo-Indians were the first to live in Illinois and arrived at the close of the last Ice Age — a time when glaciers were gone and Illinois was almost completely covered by spruce forests.

As the climate grew warmer over the next few thousand years spruces gave way to hardwood forests of ash, oak, elm, maple, birch, and hickory. Mastodons that once roamed the state became extinct. In their place, state historians said animals we still see today began to emerge, including whitetail deer, wolf, wild turkey, raccoon, and a host of riverine animals. Paleo-Indians were hunter-gatherers and their settlements can be found across Illinois. While prehistoric people were in and out of the Peoria area for centuries, Harn said there is no evidence of a large population center until a fortified village with perhaps 200 inhabitants was built in the middle 1200s at the mouth of Ten Mile Creek — about 25 miles southeast of Quail Lakes as the crow flies.

The next major change on the Illinois landscape came about 7,000 to 8,000 years ago as prairie plants began to thrive thanks to an increasingly warmer, drier climate. Some forest and marsh remained. But in the uplands, in the river bottoms, and on the flat black plains, prairie took over — tall grasses and wildflowers that spread as far as the eye could see. Those same plants also gained a foothold at Quail Lakes.

Along with the changing landscape came changes for residents. Harn and other state archaeologists term the new period of Native American culture Archaic and divide it into three sub-periods: Early (10,000 to 8,000 years ago), Middle (8,000 to 5,000 years ago), and Late Archaic (5,000 to 3,000 years ago).

Early Archaic residents were hunters and gatherers and were widely dispersed over a landscape still dominated by forest. As climate shifted and prairie spread, new resources became available and Middle Archaic people began to build permanent housing and to settle in small villages. By Late Archaic times, populations were cultivating native plants along with an early variety of gourd-like squash to supplement what they continued to hunt and gather. They also learned to live with the grass and to make the most of the wildlife that roamed the prairie.

Change came again for the next inhabitants of Illinois, the Woodland people. They lived between 800 and 3,000 years ago and, like the miners who would follow years later, the Woodland people were diggers. Their goal was not to gather coal for fires, but rather to dig pits for cooking and storage and to bury the dead. The Woodland people were the first of the Mound Builders and are credited with creating numerous burial mounds. Along with these mortuary sites, impressive ceremonial mounds appeared along major Illinois river valleys when the Mississippian culture held sway across the state from about 550 to 1,100 years ago.

Like Diane and me, these earliest indigenous residents turned to the land to grow corn in areas that were most easily tilled. Mound Builders also established extensive settlements, often along rivers. The largest Mississippian settlement in Illinois was Cahokia near present-day Collinsville, a prehistoric metropolis that covered some seven square miles.

The Mississippian people present an interesting insight into land use by Native Americans. For some time, archaeologists believed there were seven Mississippian villages at the same time along the Illinois River. "For years we thought there were populations of maybe 5,000, 6,000 or 7,000 people here in the valley [at that time]," Harn explained. But as he did more digging and studied surface details from the seven sites, Harn made a startling discovery. The Mississippian people had stayed in one location until they fouled their nest, killed the wild game nearby, and exhausted easily accessible wood and resources. Then the villagers packed up and moved.

"In the end it was simply a continuum of occupation by the same basic group. As populations wore out the soil, killed off the game and wore out the environment, everybody picked up lock stock and barrel and moved 12-15 miles and they were in a new Utopia that was untapped," Harn observed. "Indians were terrible conservationists. The longest they stayed was 60-70 years. Most [villages] lasted 30-50 years."

Although it's probable some Mound Builders spent time at Quail Lakes, no burial mounds have been found on the property. There are several in the surrounding area, though. People of the Woodland culture likely created a series of mounds in Millbrook Township in northwest Peoria County, roughly 15 miles north of Quail Lakes. Another settlement inhabited by both Archaic and Woodland cultures was found 2.5 miles northeast of Quail Lakes on a bluff overlooking Kickapoo Creek. Other smaller caches of arrowheads, axe heads, and pottery have also been found near Quail Lakes, but were not reported to state archaeologists.

The next native Illinoisans are termed Protohistoric. These people had ties to the Upper Mississippian and Oneota groups occupying northern Illinois, but they were more transient with smaller, less urban communities. They lived at a time termed the "Little Ice Age" that brought more snow and colder winters for nearly 300 years.

While bison are known to have been present in Illinois for nearly 2,400 years, scientists believe the big mammals became more common at this time. The same may have been true for elk. It's hard for me to imagine bison grazing across our Quail Lakes property. But that's not only possible, it is probable. And there can be little doubt Protohistoric people also visited Quail Lakes before they passed with barely a trace into the mists of time.

Sometime in the 1600s, tribes of the Illiniwek Confederation — an amalgamation of as many as 13 Native American tribes — first occupied large sections of central and northern Illinois. This is the Historic Period of native inhabitation, ranging from the 1500s to 1832. In central Illinois members of the confederation found a landscape of prairies and forests. Through the middle ran the Illinois River — whose fertile backwaters provided an abundance of fish and game.

Harn said the Illinois tribes may have been in this area for only a few generations before meeting French explorers in 1673. Most tribes lived in bark-covered, pole-frame log houses in villages they established in spring and summer along rivers. And they used the land. Starting prairie fires was a common practice when hunting bison — or when preparing for war with a rival tribe. Trees were cut for homes and fires. Animals fell to the bow. Land was tilled for crops.

This was the scene that greeted French missionary Pere Jacques Marquette and his fur trader companion Louis Jolliet when they paddled birch-bark canoes up the Illinois River in August and September of 1673. According to their account (a comprehensive version of which is available through the Wisconsin Historical Society), the explorers saw an Indian village on a hill and stopped, pulling their canoes to shore and drawing a crowd of natives. As far as we know, this marked the first time white Europeans met face to face with non-white natives on land that is today Illinois.

To prepare for such a moment, Marquette and Jolliet had brought cheap knives and trinkets to share with natives — a wise decision since the finery helped break the ice. Explorers came to Illinois to traverse the unsettled territory from the Great Lakes to the Gulf of Mexico. Working for King Louis XIV of France they hoped to document for French and Canadian officials what they found. They did a wonderful job. Jolliet wrote of the Illinois River:

> The river which we named for Saint Louis, which rises near the lower end of the lake of the Illinois [Peoria Lakes], seemed to me the most beautiful, and most suitable for settlement. ... The river is wide and deep, abounding in catfish and sturgeon. Game is abundant there; oxen, cows, stags, does, and turkeys are found there in greater numbers than elsewhere. For a distance of eighty leagues, I did not pass a quarter of an hour without seeing some.
>
> There are prairies three, six, ten, and 20 leagues in length, and three in width, surrounded by forests of the same extent; beyond these, the prairies begin again, so that there is as much of one sort of land as of the other. Sometimes we saw the grass very short, and, at other times, five or six feet high; hemp, which grows naturally there, reaches a height of eight feet. A settler would not there spend ten years in cutting down

and burning the trees; on the very day of his arrival, he could put his plow into the ground. And, if he had no oxen from France, he could use those of this country, or even the animals possessed by the Western Savages, on which they ride, as we do on horses.

Added Marquette:

We have seen nothing like this river [the Illinois River] that we enter, as regards its fertility of soil, its prairies and woods; its cattle, elk, deer, wildcats, bustards [Canada geese], swans, ducks, parroquets, and even beaver. There are many small lakes and rivers. That on which we sailed is wide, deep, and still, for 65 leagues.

The "parroquets" Marquette referred to were the now-extinct Carolina parakeet. Jolliet's oxen were actually bison that he envisioned settlers yoking to the plow. The "Western Savages" Marquette and Jolliet encountered were those of the Illiniwek Confederation. As history has it, the Illini (or Illinois) — which means "the men" — took possession of the state after driving out Sioux tribes and forcing the Winnebagos north. This gave the Illini possession of the rich prairies of central Illinois. Prevalent tribes in central Illinois included the Peoria, Kaskaskia, and Moingwena.

The Illini are thought to have numbered in the thousands at the time of European settlement in the 1700s according to research by Dr. Robert Warren, an anthropologist at the Illinois State Museum in Springfield and an authority on the Illinois Indians. For the most part the Illini were expert hunters, skilled with bow and arrow. And they were very nomadic. In the spring they planted crops — corn, beans, squash, and even watermelons — and established large villages. They lived in log houses. By fall they scattered to establish smaller winter villages, with smaller log houses that were more dome-shaped like wigwams. Too many people in one area made it hard to find enough game, a staple in the winter.

From 1691 to 1720, most of the Illini moved from the Starved Rock area down the Illinois River to the Peoria area. Here they found abundant fish and game and fine ground to grow crops. But the Illini did not hold sway for long over the state they named. European settlers arrived in the east and displaced tribes. As a result, members of some eastern Iroquois tribes moved west and battled the Illini. Other fights raged for years, with Sioux, Foxes, Kickapoo, Potawatomi, and other northern tribes a constant threat to the Illiniwek, who had been weakened by battles with the Iroquois.

Non-stop fighting took a toll according to Warren. Once believed to number as many as 11,000, the Illini were reduced to around 2,000 by 1760 due to war and disease. By 1765 most of the Illini had moved from the Peoria area, though remnants of the tribe remained until 1832. By 1800, the Illini may have numbered just 300.

Meanwhile, the Kickapoo Indians claimed the village of Peoria for themselves in 1768 and made it their principal settlement. At Quail Lakes, a tributary of Kickapoo Creek runs through part of the property. The Kickapoos, Potawatomi, and Peoria are thought to have been three tribes who spent the most time in Peoria County and are the most likely to have spent time hunting at Quail Lakes.

But singling out one tribe as the predominant inhabitants of Quail Lakes is difficult. Dalton talked often of interacting with Potawatomi Indians, whose language he spoke fluently. Most historic accounts are less specific, with general references to "Indians." For instance, many early settlers in Elmwood Township followed what they called "Indian trails" to reach new areas. William J. Phelps reached Peoria on Sept. 30, 1834. The next day, his son wrote, "He followed an Indian trail, on foot, to Farmington."

Tradition also has it that the mound between the towns of Elmwood and its western neighbor Yates City was a lookout spot for warring chiefs. Generations later, arrowheads, axe heads, and other Indian artifacts were common finds in fields around Elmwood. "When we were still using moldboard plows, we'd have guys running out in the fields after us to look for arrowheads," said Lynn Shissler, an Elmwood farmer.

Changes in the Native American tribal hierarchy coincided with changes in the status of Illinois — which was first established as a county in 1778 and was eventually admitted to the Union in 1818.

In 1819 the Kickapoo Indians moved west of the Mississippi River and ceded most of their lands in central Illinois. Even so, until the early 1830s, Indian tribes held sway over much of Illinois. Settlement was limited to a brave few, including John Ewalt — the first settler in Elmwood Township. Ewalt arrived on May 1, 1831, taking up residence one mile east of Quail Lakes. He came from Edgar County in east-central

Doug Oberhelman

Illinois and brought four sons, settling first near a large tract of timber. *The History of Peoria County* and the *Portrait and Biographical Album of Peoria County, Illinois* tell us the Ewalts built a cabin that year while living out of their wagon and a tent. Things must have gone well, because by the next year Ewalt brought his wife and the rest of his family to the area.

Years later, son William Dowden Ewalt told the *Elmwood Gazette* that while Native Americans were plentiful, "no trouble was experienced from them and the most friendly relations were maintained until the last one took up his line of march, westward."

John Ewalt was an exception. Most would-be settlers waited to see what would happen with the natives. Atop the watch list in central Illinois was Black Hawk, a Sauk chief who was involved in a series of skirmishes until August of 1832, when he was imprisoned at Prairie du Chien, Wisconsin.

Prior to that, Black Hawk had aligned his Sauk and Foxes with the British in the War of 1812. Then in 1816, he and 22 other Sauk leaders signed a treaty reaffirming an 1804 agreement by which they had ceded all lands east of the Mississippi River to the United States. By terms of the 1804 treaty, the Sauk and Foxes could remain in the land only until white settlers arrived. Then they were to leave for a reservation west of the Mississippi. This was not a popular treaty with the tribe and many settlers were hesitant to move into disputed lands, which included central Illinois.

Things only got worse when President John Quincy Adams proclaimed the lands open to white settlement in 1828 and ordered Native Americans to go west of the Mississippi River. Black Hawk at first refused to leave. Even after he left in 1830, he returned with several members of his tribe the following spring. Matters reached a boiling point in 1832 as blood was shed on both sides in fights between Native Americans and settlers, militiamen, and U.S. soldiers. This fighting was not lost on would-be settlers or those who were already in the area. "Many settlers along the frontiers of Northern Illinois, in dread of the untold horrors of savage warfare, fled from their lands and homes, some of them never to return," wrote Eliza Jane Shallenberger in *Stark County and its Pioneers*.

But in a three-month series of battles fought in Wisconsin and northern Illinois — including at least one in which private Avery Dalton appeared — U.S. armed forces defeated Black Hawk and held him as a prisoner of war until June 4, 1833. Also in 1833, thousands of Native Americans were invited to a gathering in Chicago where they were ordered to leave their lands between Lake Michigan and the Mississippi River. In exchange, the tribes were told they would have lands in the west, food, and clothing. The treaty was signed and Native Americans left Illinois en masse. While this was a sad period of U.S. history, it also opened Illinois and the rest of the west for an unparalleled run of prosperity.

With Black Hawk and other tribes gone, the pace of settlement increased. According to *The History of Peoria County Illinois*, the 1800 population of Illinois (not counting Native Americans) was 2,458. By 1870 that number soared to 2.5 million. A similar pattern emerged in Peoria County, whose 1840 population was just 6,153. By 1850 the population of Peoria County nearly tripled to 17,547 and by 1860 doubled again to 36,601.

One reason Ewalt, Dalton, and others like him were lured to the prairie was the rich, black topsoil. "Tickle it with a hoe, and it will laugh with a harvest," author Henry L. Kiner quoted an early settler in *The History of Henry County, Illinois*.

Similar sentiments were expressed about farmland in Peoria County. Ewalt was the first settler to break the soil in Elmwood Township and was the first in Elmwood Township to raise corn, buckwheat, winter wheat, and potatoes. In his first year he had 40 acres fenced and broken. By 1834, just three years later, he had 340 acres under cultivation and was providing grain and provisions for the next wave of settlers.

James Daugherty wrote of Ewalt, "His name has spread far and wide, as a large farmer and a hospitable man. My informant assures me that he has seen as many as 20 teams at the farm of a day, wanting supplies for themselves and their families. They were all provided for. Some had money, others had promises. It was all the same, John Ewalt supplied all their wants."

Before he died in 1869, Ewalt amassed 1,300 acres and lived in a fine, brick house. Hard work made Ewalt. But so did the land.

After Ewalt, the next settlers to arrive in Elmwood Township were Isaac Doyle and his family in May of 1832. According to numerous historical accounts, the next to come was Henry Cone in June of 1834, William J. Phelps in September of 1834, Fountain Watkins in the winter of 1835 (Watkins is buried in a tiny cemetery east of Quail Lakes), A.M. Wiley in 1835, Justus Gibbs and Rolden Pierce in 1836, and in 1837 Avery Dalton — the "grandfather" of Quail Lakes.

All were lured by the promise of prosperity, or at least a better life. Nearly all began as farmers, breaking prairie sod and fencing off a few acres. The soil they found was black and rich. A blessing, they said, though few pondered the nature of this blessing. Few knew that eons of natural events had nurtured the soil of Illinois into the world's finest.

The story of that soil starts millions of years earlier when a vast sea covered Illinois. Eventually the land rose and the sea drained away. Over time glaciers formed and, according to the Illinois Department of Natural Resources, their thick ice sheets at one point covered about 85 percent of the state during the Pleistocene Epoch (from 1.6 million to about 10,000 years ago). Only the northwest, the far southern tip, and parts of western Illinois along the Mississippi River were not glaciated. The rest of the state was reshaped by huge ice masses. As glaciers plowed across the land they flattened hills, filled valleys, and left behind a flat land with rich deposits of glacial dust, or loess. Over time, prairie grass began to grow on this flat land. Each year grasses and forbs grew tall, then died back and decayed. This created a dark, rich, swampy prairie soil.

The prairie also created an imposing blockade. Therein lies the irony of the settlement of Illinois. While prairie became a drawing card, it started as an impediment. Before farming, hunting, and coal mining could begin at Quail Lakes or anywhere else, settlers had to fight through thick stands of unfamiliar plants. That was a slow process. While tall grasses and prairie forbs have a legion of "native plant" fans today, to the 1800s farmer the stands of grass were not popular. In fact, early farmers waged war on native plants.

Imagine the surprise of settlers upon leaving wooded areas of the south only to encounter grasses that stood waist high to a man riding a horse. The plants seemed foreign and unfriendly, even frightening. For a time, European settlers even viewed the vast prairies as infertile wastelands due to the absence of trees, which were limited mainly to waterways. That's why in the earliest days of Illinois, settlers generally limited their homesteads to the edge of prairies, which typically meant along rivers.

In *The Settlement of Illinois, 1778-1830*, author Arthur Clinton Boggess quoted a 1786 letter from James Monroe to Thomas Jefferson that describes the prairies of Illinois as: "Territory [that] is miserably poor ... and that upon the Mississippi and the Illinois consists of extensive plains which have not had, from appearances, and will not have, a single bush on them for ages. The districts, therefore, within which these fall will never contain a sufficient number of inhabitants to entitle them membership in the confederacy."

There were other problems with prairie. The flat lands were often poorly drained. Insects were everywhere. So were diseases like malaria and ague. Prairie fires were a constant worry in summer, as were prairie blizzards in winter. And there was the more general fear of the unknown. Vast green expanses made settlers feel small. As 19th century author Washington Irving opined in *A Tour of the Prairies*, "To one accustomed to it there is something inexpressibly lonely in the solitude of the prairie. The loneliness of a forest seems nothing to it. There the view is shut in by the trees and the imagination is left to picture some livelier scene beyond. But here we have the immense extent to landscape without a sign of human existence. We have the consciousness of being far, far beyond the bounds of human habitation." No wonder nearly all land with timber in Illinois was claimed by 1835 while prairie tracts could be purchased from the government for another 20 years.

Vast, yes. Frightening, yes. But infertile? Nothing was further from the truth. Soils developed by thousands of years of plant decay were among the world's most fertile, as today's impressive yields of corn and soybeans attest. Below that rich, black prairie soil was another source of riches — abundant seams of black coal, formed thousands of years ago before the grass took over. Before settlers could mine the coal, they had to tame the prairie, which towered above and below the ground.

The tallest of prairie grasses was big bluestem, which covered much of Illinois and stretched skyward as much as nine feet. Big bluestem was the most common grass on the plains of Illinois and in 1989 was legally declared the state's official prairie grass. The towering height of big bluestem limited other plants by shading them from the sun. In places this led to vast stands of the grass — also known as turkey foot for its unique seed head — which to settlers probably seemed like an impenetrable wall of green, blue or purple depending on the time of year. As Irving wrote, "It was like struggling through forests of cast iron."

Quail Lakes was no doubt blanketed with big bluestem and other native grasses and flowers. "Peoria County is largely prairie. The timber is confined to the bluffs, ravines, and river bottoms," noted the 1880 *History of Peoria County*. This was particularly true in western reaches of the county, which include Quail Lakes. As the 1902 *History of Peoria County* explained, "The prairies are usually small, the most extensive ones being those in the western and northern portions of the county and extending over the highest lands between the water courses."

Years after settlement, a few patches of prairie lingered. In an article entitled *Boys of Elmwood*, Stanley DuBois wrote about growing up in the town of Elmwood, which was founded in 1854. "It was set down at the edge of a prairie, lovely for location. For miles and miles, north and west, to a world round horizon, those prairies in summer time were covered with a kaleidoscopic carpet of agricultural verdure, or blossomed brilliantly with a wealth of wild flowers and grasses. These prairies were dotted here and there with the modest, plain and mostly poor little farm houses and farm buildings of the pioneers; buds of a future harvest of wealth, comfort and high civilization, which is not surpassed anywhere in the United States."

Part of the attraction of Quail Lakes to Diane and me was its relatively quiet and isolated location at the western edge of Peoria County. We can picture such memories of nearly 200 years ago.

In addition to big bluestem, as many as 30 other grasses were found in the prairie, including little bluestem, gama grass, Indian grass, switchgrass, and prairie cord grass. All typically stood 3 feet or taller and were joined by as many as 250 species of wildflowers and smaller sedges. The prairie that had taken over nearly 8,000 years earlier at one time covered more than 250 million acres of North America — from the Gulf of Mexico into Canada. That included nearly all of Illinois except for the far southern reaches.

As recently as the 1820s, biologists believe the tallgrass prairie of Illinois spanned 22 million acres — or more than 60 percent of the entire state. In that prairie lived as many as 851 species of plants, according to the *Illinois Plant Information Network*, as well as 60 species of mammals, 300 species of birds, and more than 1,000 different insects.

Prairie held sway until the 1800s, when settlers began plowing. W.E. Phelps, son of the third settler in Elmwood Township, recalled spending the entire summer of 1851 breaking prairie sod. "I followed a three-horse breaking plow the entire season," he wrote. Many others did the same. Settlers were industrious, driven by necessity and by a desire to get ahead in life. Growing crops was their best bet, but required hard work. Breaking the dense roots of the prairie plants was a sweaty, time-consuming task some termed "deviling."

Naturalist Donald Culross Peattie called prairie "the empire of locked roots" in homage to the roots of native plants that sometimes reached 10-15 feet down into the soil. The best time to plow this dense sod was May through July, since this was the surest way to kill plants and prevent rooting. But the fertile ground was sticky and the towering prairie made working the soil doubly difficult. Cast-iron plows of the time quickly became clogged with dirt and required constant attention.

The story of prairie breaking owes several chapters to Illinois ingenuity and to technological innovations. Likely the most significant step toward mass settlement of the prairie was John Deere's 1837 invention of a self-scouring, steel-bladed plow in Grand Detour, Illinois. With his "Plow That Broke the Plains" a settler could now break virgin prairie

My father Ernie Oberhelman and I were all smiles while posing for this picture on the dock at Cabin Lake.

sod.

As a child I remember going to Grand Detour with my dad, Ernie, who was a salesman at a John Deere dealership in the northern Illinois towns of Huntley and Harvard. He was a farm-equipment salesman and would always bring machinery home. I can remember crawling on those machines and riding on the tractors he brought home to show me, my mother Donna, and my sister Lori. That's what started my fascination with big equipment.

One thing Dad never told me, though, was that an Illinois blacksmith named John Lane is believed to have been the first to come up with a steel plow. As the story goes, Lane cut three lengths of steel from an old saw. He fastened two of them to his moldboard plow. The third piece was attached to the share, the piece that cuts the furrow. This high-grade steel did a better job of scouring itself and shedding sticky soil than cast-iron plows. At just about the same time, a fellow blacksmith named John Deere was also working on developing a better plow. Deere not only designed a plow, he received a patent for the invention. The rest is agricultural history.

With Deere's invention settlers were no longer plagued by gobs of black, prairie soil sticking to their plow. Nor did they need huge teams of horses or oxen to break a field. Deere's plow made everything easier. Demand was good from the start, even though the earliest plows sold for $10 to $12, which at the time was quite a sum. From just 10 plows in 1839, John Deere's sales soared. By 1842 he made 100 plows. By 1843 he made 400. By 1849, one year after moving to Moline, Deere and a work force of 16 produced 2,136 plows. By 1855 production topped 10,000 plows.

Railroads were also spreading into Illinois. The relationship between railroad and plow was complimentary. Deere's plow allowed farmers to raise crops — railroads allowed farmers to ship grain to urban markets.

Improvements in drainage also helped farmers deal with the notoriously wet and often poorly drained prairie soils. The first efforts to use tile drains in Illinois were in Champaign County in 1858. Tile factories sprang up in Joliet and Chicago, but tiling prices were too high for most farmers. In 1878, the Illinois General Assembly authorized creating drainage districts with taxing powers. By the 1880s efforts to install drainage tile in fields spread, with costs sometimes running $40 per acre

Quail Lakes & Coal

Here is a photo from 1913 showing a Holt Caterpillar Tractor pulling a Holt Combined Harvester in the state of Washington. Photo courtesy of Caterpillar Inc. Corporate Archives.

— or nearly three times the price of the land itself.

"From 1870 to 1920, ditching and tile draining transformed these lands into the most productive farms in the corn belt. Wet prairies rapidly lost their persistent, strongly negative image. In a remarkably short time they appeared to rise from rags to riches," writes Hugh Prince in *Wetlands of the American Midwest.* Levees were also built to hold back floodwaters in fertile bottomlands. And the spread of cheap barbwire fencing after the Civil War also helped, as finding enough wood to fence prairie fields had been a problem because trees were scarce.

By the way, the late 1870s is around the same time that Caterpillar founders Benjamin Holt and Daniel Best were perfecting their innovative combined harvesters for wheat farmers on the West Coast. While Caterpillar isn't viewed as an agricultural company today, that's how the company started. Both Holt and Best worked to perfect steam traction engine tractors, but the heavy, steam-driven machinery of the time often bogged down in wet soils. So Holt turned to a belted crawler track as a solution. In 1904 he started testing his track-type tractor prototype — the Holt Junior Steam Traction Engine No. 77 — in a slough in Stockton, California. The steamer's rear wheels were replaced by a set of tracks made of malleable link belts with wooden blocks as treads. Not long after that, Holt's company photographer Charles Clements called the machine a "Caterpillar." The rest is heavy equipment history.

Incidentally, Peter Holt — a great-grandson of Benjamin Holt — is a good friend of ours and lives in San Antonio, Texas. He has quite an impressive collection of Holt memorabilia and also happens to own a very successful Cat dealership in Texas.

Fueled by all this new technology, farmers kept putting more ground into production. By the early 1900s prairies were all but gone. Settlement happened so rapidly and efficiently that in about 50 years, most of what had been 22 million acres of native plants was converted to agricultural use. "The tender plants, the sweet flowers, the fragrant fruits, the busy insects, all the swarming lives which had been native here for untold centuries were utterly destroyed ... [The prairie] had vanished as if it had all been dreamed ... The pigeons, the plover, the chickens, the vultures, the cranes, the wolves — all gone — all gone!" wrote Hamlin Garland in *Boy Life on the Prairie*.

Today the Illinois Department of Natural Resources says less than 1 percent of the Illinois tallgrass prairie remains, much of it at sites like Quail Lakes that have been restored by conservation-minded land stewards. To some, the loss is lamentable. To settlers fighting to survive, there was no other option. Not unlike the treatment of the Native American, the plowing of the prairie was a sad piece of history. Yet the makeover of prairie into rich agricultural land contributed mightily to the success of today's America.

Breaking the prairie allowed agriculture to spread rapidly across the Midwest and Peoria County. In 1850, the county produced just over 1 million bushels of corn according to *The History of Peoria County Illinois*. By 1860 corn production had more than doubled. By 1880 Peoria County topped 4 million bushels of corn. Similar gains were seen for potatoes and oats, which went from 138,718 bushels in 1850 to 733,467 bushels by 1880. And the land in Elmwood Township was among the best around, with assessed land value of $125,662 in 1851, third best in Peoria County.

The first men to break the sod of Quail Lakes were Isaac Doyle and Avery Dalton. Doyle was the second settler of Elmwood Township, arriving on May 1, 1832. He owned a portion of Section 30 and in 1833 was named the first justice of the peace. Of him, little else is written. Not so Dalton, a character for the ages who was called Peoria County's "Grand Old Man" by the *Peoria Herald-Transcript* when he celebrated his 100th birthday.

Avery Dalton's life was the stuff of today's movie scripts, though at the time he lived his story was not so uncommon. He was born on December 20, 1808, in Pittsylvania County, Virginia, and was one of nine children of Samuel and Ludah Dalton. His father Samuel was a soldier in the war of 1812 and received a government pension. Little is written about the work life of Samuel Dalton in either *The History of Peoria County* or the *Portrait and Biographical Album of Peoria County, Illinois*, two sources we used to retell Avery Dalton's life story.

What we do know is that eventually Samuel Dalton headed west with his nine children, traveling with one horse and an ox cart to Highland County in southwestern Ohio. Avery walked while his mother and younger siblings rode in the cart. At night Avery and his father kept watch around the campfire for Native Americans or wild animals. While they evaded wild cats, wolves, and angry Iroquois, the Dalton's trip did not end well. Shortly after reaching Ohio in 1827, Ludah Dalton died. After her death, the family broke up.

By 1830 Avery, now 22, was ready to head west again. This time he joined a family leaving Ohio for Illinois. To earn his keep, Avery took care of the family's baby and drove two cows. He arrived in the area of Peoria along the Illinois River, which in those days was a common stopping point for visitors to central Illinois. Actually, Peoria had been a waypoint for longer than that, as Native Americans had for years set up villages along the fertile waters of Peoria's two lakes. When Dalton arrived, various tribes were still in the area. Though it's hard to imagine, Illinois was part of the western frontier as recently as 1830. Years later Dalton told the *Peoria Herald-Transcript*, "There was not many white people in Peoria or in the country those days. Just a few houses. I walked from Peoria to Marchant's Settlement the whole way and did not find a house the entire distance. There were no roads cut and it was a wild walk."

Marchant's Settlement — named for Abraham Marchant, the first pioneer in the area according to the *History of Fulton County Illinois* — is the present-day town of Farmington in the northeast corner of Fulton County. Dalton arrived with 10 cents, a rifle, and an axe. He earned the money by carrying pumpkins during the journey west from Ohio. Once in Fulton County he worked for a farmer and earned three bushels of oats per day. Since there was no market for the grain, he held it for a month before selling the oats for 37 cents. How he made ends meet in the meantime we do not know, though it's a safe bet Dalton shot his share of squirrels, deer, and turkeys to fill the stew pot.

In the spring of 1831, Dalton hired out for $10 per month to a farmer who lived six miles northeast of Knoxville. According to the *Portrait and Biographical Album*, Dalton had to walk 16 miles and cross the Spoon River to reach his place of work. "There being no bridges there was no other way but to wade [across the river] or miss the opportunity of making some money. The latter alternative was not to be thought of, so divesting himself of his clothing, Mr. Dalton held it above his head and walked boldly into the water which, the month being March, was so cold it almost took his breath away." For his efforts, Dalton was rewarded with $13.50 in silver half-dollars.

Obviously, Dalton was eager to earn money. By all accounts he was a hard worker and a true character, if historic references are reliable. It was said of him that, "While he built many schoolhouses in his lifetime, he never attended one." Instead he was blessed with frontier wisdom.

Among his many endearing traits was his skill as a hunter. Dalton said often that he could shoot whitetail deer and wild turkeys right out of his backyard to provide food for his children. Indeed, according to the *Portrait and Biographical Album*: "Uncle Avery, as he is familiarly called, has perhaps killed more deer than any man in this region, while scores of wild turkeys and other game fell before his rifle in the days when this section was all wild woods. He speaks the Indian language fluently and many are the stories he can tell of frontier life. He is an uncompromising temperance man, has never used tobacco or sworn an oath. His motto is 'as you mete out to others so it shall be meted out to you.'"

Uncle Avery's skill with a rifle was not uncommon at the time. In a speech to the Congregational Church of Elmwood later reprinted in the *Elmwood Gazette*, W.E. Phelps discussed the hunting skills of settlers. "Those early settlers were most of them great hunters. They were nearly all good marksmen, and not a few of them were expert shots. Woe to the squirrel that peeps over a limb at Uncle Avery Dalton, even now in his 85th year."

Wild game remained relatively abundant until the prairie disappeared. One of the best accounts of those early days in central Illinois is from H. Clay Merritt's fascinating *The Shadow of a Gun*. Merritt came west from Connecticut largely to hunt the wild game of which he'd heard so much. His arrival six miles outside of Henry, Illinois in June of 1855 did not disappoint.

"Prairie chickens were everywhere on the prairie," he wrote. "We could scare up five or six flocks, possibly a dozen when going through one stubble field, and the flocks were large. It was no use to kill many, so we contented ourselves with a limited number, as many as the family could eat and as many as we could give away to our neighbors. ... As the season became later, quails appeared in large numbers, more plentifully around the thickets and along the water courses, but plenty enough in the corn fields. ... I went down below Henry on the east side the latter part of October, and there the quantity of ducks to be seen passed all records."

While Merritt hunted for the market, most shot wild game for the dinner table. That included Dalton, who hunted squirrels at age 100 and generally enjoyed a life that included plenty of hunting, fishing, and good living. Interesting living, too. Dalton was said to have shaken hands with Potawatomi chiefs. Even at age 98 he could still sing songs learned from natives he met as a youth. During a particularly hard winter in 1830 he shared corn with Native Americans who had not set aside enough food. He cast his first vote for president for Andrew Jackson in 1832 and voted for 21 more presidents before he died. He also served in the Black Hawk War of 1832 as a private in Captain David W. Barnes' company and fought in the battle of Stillman's Run. At the time of his death Dalton was thought to be the last remaining veteran of that war.

Nearly all of Dalton's good living was on Section 19, the ground that would later be surface mined for coal and become part of our Quail Lakes. Other settlers also moved into the area and by 1873, the Peoria County plat book shows many names on the land of Quail Lakes: W. Threw, J. Conklin, I. Doyle, J.M. Wiley, A. McGrail, J. Ewalt, E. Watkins, H&D Jackson, J. Parsell, C.W. Miller, J.W. Snyder, and A. Reed.

Still Dalton was arguably the most memorable. He called the area he settled Lost Prairie for a little patch of prairie in the midst of timber on the north end of the section. On Sept. 10, 1835, Dalton had married his wife Delilah Dalton, who was his second cousin — which was not uncommon at the time, particularly among settlers. She was also said to be

Doug Oberhelman

Someone peers out of the front door of Avery Dalton's homestead, which began as a log home and years later included the brick addition shown in this picture. Photo courtesy of Bruce Howard.

a hard-working woman, who understood the requirements of frontier living. Less than two years later in 1837 the Daltons bought 40 acres on Section 19, selling their last cow to pay for the purchase.

Years later at Delilah's funeral, W.E. Phelps read an account of her life that was published in the *Elmwood Gazette* and included the following: "We today have very little conception of the conditions which surrounded them and the privations they had to endure. The wigwam poles were still standing in the Indian camps not half a mile away. The country was a wilderness, only here and there a settler's cabin and a feeble attempt to cultivate a little patch of land. When they came into this house there were no windows or doors; the logs had not yet been chunked; the floor was of puncheons and the roof of clapboards. It was four years before they had a chair. They sat on stools and benches. A wide puncheon smoothed with an ax and supported on rough legs served as a table, and shelves on the wall answered for cupboards and closets."

Be it ever so humble, there's no place like home. Over time, Dalton added a fine brick addition next door to his log home. For their 50th wedding anniversary in 1885, newspaper accounts indicate the Daltons served a spread that was the talk of the township: a calf, two hogs, two turkeys and 12 chickens. Avery lived there until 1905, when he moved two miles north to Elmwood to live with his son Cicero. Around his 100th birthday, Dalton reminisced about the past. "We always had deer in our yard, and at night I heard the wild turkeys gobble. I used to shoot them from my back door. We always had venison. We have game laws now, but we used to have game laws of our own, and never thought of killing any game out of season as we call it."

Things are not so different today. Well, game laws are confusing enough that even a man with frontier wisdom might have trouble deciphering them. But deer still wander through Quail Lakes. Diane and I see and hear wild turkeys in the spring. Other wild animals are also abundant, attracted in part by the deep, clear lakes left behind when surface mining was done ... in part by native prairie grasses and forbs we have planted in areas once mined for coal.

It would be interesting to compare notes with Avery Dalton on his old property. No doubt he would be pleased to see the lakes created by surface mines, since lakes were rare in Avery's day — a time when fishing and swimming was

Avery Dalton's tombstone in Elmwood Cemetery includes the inscription, "Pvt Stillman's Bn Ill. Mtd. Vols Black Hawk War" and stands next to a newer headstone inscribed with the dates of his birth and death.

done in a creek or river. Beyond that are plenty of questions for Avery Dalton whose answers are less clear. Have there always been coveys of quail along the creek in the northeast corner of the section? Where were the old deer bedding areas? Where did the wild turkeys roost in the

Doug Oberhelman

1830s? What about the ducks and geese? Did they spend long in the area while migrating south?

There's no way to know. Diane and I can only dream about life in the 1830s and about how priceless a conversation with Uncle Avery would be. However we are content to leave something for others that will be a story 150 years from now, not unlike Avery's legacy.

When he died on July 15, 1913, newspapers printed glowing tributes to Avery Dalton, including this one from Dr. E. A. Taylor of Chicago: "He was the last of that noble band of early pioneers who planted the seed of civilization on the virgin soil of Illinois; who lived and labored for the common welfare, and with brave hearts and honest hands wrought the things necessary for their comfort, seeking not the vestiges of fortune nor the fallacy of fame, but striving always for the approval of their conscience rather than for the plaudits of the throng. Brave men of blessed memory! We shall not see their like again!"

No question, Dalton was industrious. While the challenges I faced can't compare to what Avery endured, Diane sees a similarity in the story of my arrival in Peoria. I came to Peoria to work for Caterpillar as a credit analyst in the treasury department in 1975 after graduating from Millikin University. I lived in a tiny furnished apartment that was half of a two-story garage and that rented for $75 per month. I focused on working hard to pay off college loans and the loan I took out to buy my first car, a baby blue Pontiac Grand Prix. I was willing to work hard, although at the time I never dreamed I would one day become Chairman and CEO of Caterpillar.

It's hard to imagine Avery could have imagined the way his life would play out, either. He settled in Illinois with pennies, an axe, and a rifle. Not long after arriving he purchased 40 acres, a colt, four sheep, three cows, and nine hogs. Before he died he had a farm of more than 400 acres. Along the way Dalton harvested wild game and worked the land to make a living. He raised a bountiful crop from the fine black soil of Quail Lakes. He was respected by neighbors and was viewed as a pillar of the community. And as we shall see, he discovered another source of black gold on the property.

CHAPTER TWO
ILLINOIS MINING COMES OF AGE

For the pioneers in Illinois, coal was an afterthought. Before they could focus on mining, settlers had to build homes and fences, and break the prairie sod. The workload was immense and required long days and backbreaking labor. The first and most obvious jobs were to work the rich black topsoil and then to find a source of energy to keep warm and to cook food. So after long days of planting and plowing, settlers cut and split wood or gathered logs and sticks. Some burned sod. Or buffalo chips. Or hay. Or corn cobs. These were not the most efficient energy sources available, though. And it wasn't long before underground riches began to attract attention, as well.

That settlers sought out coal is no surprise. As the World Coal Institute has so capably documented, coal has always captivated us. There's no understating the role of coal as an energy source through world history, as Justin Wickett noted in "Coal in Human History." The Chinese used coal around 1000 B.C. to smelt copper. Greek philosopher Aristotle wrote about a dark charcoal-like rock. There were coal cinders among Roman ruins in England. And coal was central to the Industrial Revolutions in England and the United States in the 1700s and 1800s. Native Americans also used coal. Hopi Indians are said to have used coal to bake clay pottery in the 1300s and in the 1760s Nanticoke Indians of Pennsylvania used anthracite coal as a source of energy and for jewelry.

Surprisingly, archaeological research indicates European settlers were the first to tap Illinois' rich coal veins. "We know [Native Americans] knew of coal. But we haven't ever found any clinker. They never used it," emphasized Alan Harn of Dickson Mounds Museum, shaking his head in bafflement. "I've pondered that and we've talked among ourselves about that. Why? They used everything else. Things you would never think of they used. You would think somebody would have picked up a piece of coal and said, 'Let's heat it up in the fire and cook something over it.' And then find out the thing glowed forever. And yet up

Coal Creek where I am there are coal seams exposed and there probably always were coal seams exposed. And we never found any [in archaeological excavations]. We don't find objects made out of coal. I don't know. I think two or three people have tried to look at that, and without any evidence anywhere it's an immediate dead end."

That's surprising, since the ready availability of coal was no secret. As Harn said, exposed coal seams were visible to the naked eye across Illinois. In 1673, Marquette and Jolliet had written about coal outcrops they saw along the Illinois River near the present-day city of Utica. They listed the coal deposits as "charbon de terre" on a map of the Illinois River. Researchers believe that is the first mention of coal in the United States by Europeans, though future explorers were also quick to note the black coal they encountered. Father Louis Hennepin wrote of a "cole mine" along the Illinois River in 1689. French explorer Robert de LaSalle wrote a letter in 1680 in which he referred to the Illinois River and said, "There are Coal-Pits on that River."

Coal discoveries were not limited to Illinois. The critical role of coal is a prominent theme in settlement of the United States, as has been traced by The National Energy Laboratory (NETL), a part of the U.S. Department of Energy. In 1701 Huguenot settlers on the James River in Virginia found coal near what is now Richmond. Mining continued on a small scale through the early 1700s, with colonial farmers digging beds that were exposed on the surface. They would sell coal they dug in bushel baskets for use as a heating source.

Gradually, new uses were found for this abundant natural resource. By the time of the Revolutionary War, coal was used to make shot, shells, and other war items. Around that same time, mining was taking place in hillsides in Pennsylvania and elsewhere. According to NETL, Baltimore, Maryland began to light its streets with combustible gas made from coal in 1816. Then in 1830 the American-built, coal-burning locomotive Tom Thumb debuted in Maryland. In the years that followed, all locomotive engines burning wood for power were converted to coal burning.

No wonder then that finding coal was on the minds of many as they moved west into new territory. No wonder most journals and reports from settlers in Illinois or just passers-through mentioned the state's abundant supply. Lewis C. Beck's *A Gazetteer of Illinois and Missouri* in 1823 made clear reference to the available Prairie State coal. While writing of the Illinois River, Beck said, "Coal is very abundant on this stream." Of the Spoon River it was written, "Coal, of a very fine quality, is abundant on the banks of this stream and will be valuable, on account of the scarcity of timber, particularly in the northern part of the military tract." At its closest point, Spoon River flows within eight miles to the northwest of Quail Lakes.

Closer yet is Kickapoo Creek, a tributary of which flows through the property. Beck also admired coal deposits along the Kickapoo. "On the banks of this stream is an extensive bed of coal, which furnished fuel to the garrison and the inhabitants of Peoria. The stratum is about 12 or 14 feet below the surface, and is overlaid by slate, limestone and sandstone."

It's safe to say word of Kickapoo coal reached the ears of some settlers who came to Elmwood Township. So when the crops were harvested and the cold days of winter arrived, settlers picked at coal outcroppings. Among those was Avery Dalton, who scratched at several exposed seams around his Lost Prairie settlement. That tradition carried on well into the 1970s, according to Jim Grimm, a worker and superintendent for Midland Coal Company, the firm that mined Quail Lakes. "That's what some farmers did in the winters. They worked these dog holes in the side of the hills. When they were not farming in the winter they were coal miners. That's why we had a lot of [employees] when I came here that had farms. During the winter they would just find some exposed coal and dig back in there to get what they needed for the winter. It's not like a big underground mine. Just smaller laterals and digs. Or dog holes, we called them."

Coal from those earliest mining efforts went to blacksmiths or was used around the house. But with every passing year, coal became more important to our developing nation. As demand increased, so did mining in Illinois. With good reason. The Illinois Basin coal seam — one of America's four major coal basins — covers nearly 37,000 square miles in Illinois, Indiana, and western Kentucky.

Coal deposits here were formed more than 300 million years ago. Mats of plants accumulated in swamps and formed peat. This layer of peat was compressed into coal over millions of years and created more than 75 seams ranging from a few inches to 10 feet thick. In places

Doug Oberhelman

those coal seams cover thousands of square miles. No wonder coal has been mined in 73 of 102 Illinois counties and more than 4,500 mines have been documented since 1810, according to *Geology of Illinois* by the Illinois State Geological Survey.

Those first commercial mines in 1810 were along the banks of the Big Muddy River near Murphysboro according to the Illinois Department of Commerce and Economic Opportunity (IDCEO). Coal scratched from the river bluffs in Jackson County was sent on flatboats down the Big Muddy, into the Mississippi River and eventually on to New Orleans. Mining spread rapidly across the state as settlers began to move into new areas and homes and industries sprang up. By 1833, Illinois coal production stood at 6,000 tons statewide. The first underground mining operation in Illinois is thought to have been in Belleville in 1848. Around that same time in the 1850s, railroads began spreading into Illinois to make the distribution of coal easier. As more tracks went down, more coal came up. In 1844, Illinois topped 120,000 tons. By 1859, tonnage was at 530,000. By 1864, IDCEO said Illinois topped one million tons for the first time.

The importance of coal only kept growing. In fact, it's hard to imagine a developing America without coal. Our abundant natural resource touched the lives of so many people in so many ways in the 1800s that it's accurate to say coal was a necessity of life. By the end of the 19th century, people used coal for light and warmth and their homes were filled with products delivered via coal-fired locomotives. Even many of their jobs depended on coal, since the black gold provided power for steam engines, forges, and furnaces of all sorts.

Certainly coal was critical to the steel industry after about 1875 when coke — a product of burning coal — replaced wood charcoal in blast furnaces used in the steel industry. Demand kept increasing after Thomas Edison built the first coal-fired electrical power generating station in 1882 to provide electricity to residents of New York City. No wonder that by the 1880s, Peoria County's coal deposits were widely known. As noted in *The History of Peoria County*, "The great geological feature of Peoria County consists in its coal measures, which are co-extensive with its borders. ... At no place in Illinois, or perhaps the world, can coal be mined and brought to market so cheaply as in this county."

Quail Lakes & Coal

That quote is from 1880, just 13 years after the first shaft mines were built in the autumn of 1867 near Elmwood and at a time when coal could be delivered to consumers in Peoria for about $1.50 per ton. But the first known mining in the Elmwood area goes back well before that to 1838 on land belonging to W.J. Phelps. According to an account by W.E. Phelps in 1904, "My father discovered coal in a small vein on the southeast corner of section 18, the old homestead, in 1838. It was obtained in small quantities for blacksmiths' use, by stripping off the overlaying surface. Other deposits were found, and gradually coal stoves were introduced, for heating purposes. For years all the mining was done by drifting into the side hills. In 1866, associated with Mr. James Lee, I put down the first shaft in this vicinity, on the southeast of 18, and worked it by horsepower." Section 18 borders Quail Lakes and it's fair to say those mines likely crossed under our property. That first seam of coal Phelps mined is just north of where Avery Dalton started his mine.

Even so, early coal mining in Peoria County was fairly limited. The U.S. Census Report for 1840 credits coal mining in Peoria County with just 12,000 bushels and eight men employed. That would change. By 1880 Peoria County produced 273,640 tons to rank seventh among Illinois counties. In those days, most mines in Illinois were shallow shafts and consisted of a fairly crude method of "room-and-pillar" by which the mines were supported. This involved leaving a portion of the coal seam to support the roof of the room being mined. In other cases, wooden beams were built to support the roof of the mine shaft.

As coal demand continued to increase, so did mining. By 1900 there were more than 900 underground mines in Illinois according to *Illinois Coal Mining Investigations*. As more people mined they found creative new ways to gather coal. In areas where coal seams were fairly shallow, operators began to explore the idea of removing overburden — the surface soils and rocks — to uncover coal.

Most believe the first surface mining operation in the United States started in the mid-1860s west of Danville. In summer, miners used hand plows and mule-drawn scrapers to strip away the overburden of rock, dirt, and shale covering. Then in winter they would mine the coal, hauling it away in wheelbarrows and carts.

From those humble beginnings, surface mining steadily became more productive thanks largely to technological improvements. In 1855 in coal fields near Danville, Wright and Wallace used a wooden dredge with wheels that had a 50-foot boom according to the book *Surface Mining*. William S. Otis also helped spread surface mining with his 1838 invention of the steam shovel. The first recorded use of a steam shovel to mine for coal was in 1877 near Pittsburg, Kansas. The idea made so much sense that within a few years, steam shovels could be found in mines across the United States.

In Illinois, dragline steam shovels replaced horse scrapers in about 1900, according to *Illinois Coal Mining Investigations*. Standard shovels were substituted for the dragline and were replaced by revolving steam shovels in 1910. The first true stripping shovel started work in 1911 in the Mission Field near Danville. This steam-powered shovel had a 65-foot boom and a dipper that could hold 3.5 cubic yards. The shovel ran on rail lines and could operate in 20-30 feet of overburden.

As far as actual mining practices, the Illinois Geological Survey reported, "The methods of stripping now employed in the district differ [from earlier methods] in the path which the shovel follows while digging, in the manner in which the top soil is removed from the shale overlying the coal, and in the disposal of the soil." Those same changes have remained at the heart of surface mining ever since.

Notably absent from the 1915 account of surface mining is any discussion of reclaiming mined property. Instead, as coal was mined, topsoil, rock, and clay were washed or pushed into the pit from the next area to be mined. There was no thought of saving topsoil or bulldozing ridges. Miners got the coal out as fast as possible and moved on to the next seam. The concept of land stewardship as we know it today was not the focus for most people or companies— the race to grow the U.S. economy was in high gear.

Future innovations included the use of electricity to power surface-mining equipment in about 1912. Walking draglines debuted in the late 1930s. Power shovels worked from the floor of a mine pit, moving slowly on steel treads along the coal they exposed. Operators would use a shovel dipper to take bites into the overburden along walls of the pit. The machine would then pivot and deposit overburden on the other side of the pit, creating a series of ridges.

Draglines operated in a different manner. They set up on the surface edge of a pit, above the coal, and dropped huge buckets down to the overburden below. Operators would fill the bucket by dragging it back toward the machine using lines or cables — hence the name dragline. Eventually, operators would increasingly turn to draglines over shovels, as the longer booms made it easier to move overburden a greater distance.

Neither the dragline nor the shovel removed the coal from a pit, though. That job fell to smaller shovels and front-end loaders, which today might include the massive Cat 994F Wheel Loader, which has a bucket capacity of up to 47 cubic yards and is assembled only in Illinois. Not so the early machines, which had limited capacity. The first steam shovels could handle just one cubic yard of material. By the start of World War II, only a few machines in the surface-mine industry had a capacity of up to 35 cubic yards. That began to change as demand for coal increased.

Coal mined in Vermilion County in the earliest days brought 40 to 50 cents per ton once loaded on railroad cars and the daily output was about 300 tons. Yet the spread of surface mining to other parts of Illinois was at first slow. By 1920, just 0.6 percent of the bituminous coal mined in Illinois came from surface mines and all of that was from Vermilion County. Then in the 1920s, advances in stripping equipment helped the practice spread — first to Perry and Williamson counties, then to Fulton, Jackson, Saline, and Knox. By 1930, 11.9 percent of Illinois coal came from surface mines. By 1940 the total had increased to 27.25 percent and by 1953 stood at 36.29 percent according to annual reports by the Illinois Department of Mines and Minerals.

Surface mining would not come to Peoria County and to Elmwood on a large scale until much later. But mining operations expanded well beyond merely scratching into side hills. W.J. Phelps dug the first shaft mine in the Elmwood area in 1866 and organized the Elmwood Coal Company. Other settlers in the Elmwood area followed suit, including Avery Dalton. Vertical shafts typically led to a coal seam 40-60 feet below ground. Wooden beams held up the ceilings of horizontal shafts from which the coal was mined.

Improvements came rapidly. "In 1867 we put down a shaft nearer town on the southwest of section 17, and put in a set of steam hoisting machinery. Two years later, we put down another shaft near by, connecting the two, and turning the first into an escapement shaft, supposed to be the first one in the state, furnishing absolute security to the men below," wrote W.E. Phelps in the April 7, 1904 issue of the *Elmwood Gazette*.

The boom in coal mining of the 1800s paralleled a boom in industry in Elmwood. "In 1869 the Elmwood Coal Company built a narrow gauge railroad to the mines and fitted up shipping and retail yards in the village," Phelps explained. "The foundry and machine shop was started in 1869. The Elmwood paper manufacturing company was organized in 1867. A steam brick plant was also put in in 1867."

Coal operations expanded according to the *History of Peoria County*: "In the Autumn of 1869 a tramway a little more than a mile long, laid with sixteen pound tee rail, was constructed and a coal yard opened in the village. This track was also connected with the railroad chutes for coaling engines, and also with the side track for shipping coal in car loads. A year or so later a track was run into the engine room of the paper mill, furnishing it with fuel direct from the mine." As has been true throughout the history of our country, having cheap, abundant sources of energy encouraged the growth of industry.

The Dalton family did its share of mining at Quail Lakes. Roscoe Dalton, the grandson of Avery Dalton and son of James Dalton, provided an interesting account in his posthumously published memoir, *Memories of a Prairie Boyhood*. Roscoe Dalton grew up in the log house that his grandfather first built and wrote about mining on the family property:

> Then [in 1904], when I was 12 years old, Father dug a shaft down 55 feet to the number six vein of coal (which is called soft coal) and had a horse to lift the cars of coal to the top and then dump them on the platform made of planks. Then some people had horses and wagons and came and bought the coal. Some went into Elmwood and the farmers came from all around to get coal. Well, Dad got an old upright steam engine — one that had to be pulled with horses. The steam engine was to run a pump to keep the water out of the mine. My job was to fire this engine and keep up steam to run the pump. That mine played out and then we put down another shaft, or mine, down to the number five vein of coal. This shaft was 125 feet down and Dad got a big steam boiler and got an old engine that was on a boat and he made it into a

Quail Lakes & Coal

A worker pauses at the site of the Dalton coal mine, located on what is now the northeast corner of Quail Lakes. Photo courtesy of Bruce Howard.

A large smokestack towers over the Dalton family coal mine. Photo courtesy of Bruce Howard.

hoisting engine to pull the cars of coal up to the top to dump them on |the| platform. I used to keep the boiler fired to keep up steam and ran the hoisting engine by myself.

The same thing was happening across Peoria County. In an article for

55

the April 2012 issue of *InterBusiness Issues*, Marilyn J. Leyland reported, "By 1935, the secretary of the Fuel Merchants Association of Peoria noted that the coal industry furnished the livelihood of one out of 10 families in the Peoria District. The 1934 Coal Report showed 89 operating mines in 'those parts of Peoria and Tazewell counties adjacent to the city,' employing 2,387 union miners, plus owners, superintendents, maintenance men, truckers and office employees. City directories of the era showed 55 dealers or individuals as retail coal merchants. An estimated 900 to 1,000 independent trucks hauled coal to homes, schools, stores and industrial plants during Peoria's coal peak."

The coal that kept Peoria and the Daltons busy eventually attracted major companies. Consider the names involved in mining at Quail Lakes, some which jump right off the pages of American entrepreneurial history. Guggenheim. Henry Huttleston Rogers. Standard Oil. And Peabody Coal.

First Peabody Coal, which has had a mining presence in Illinois since 1883. In the 1880s, 24-year-old company founder Francis S. Peabody and a partner hitched up their team of mules to a wagon and delivered coal to homes and small businesses in Chicago. A Yale University graduate, Peabody had at first hoped to practice law. When that career choice failed he turned to the equally messy business of coal — only with much cleaner results. From humble roots Peabody Coal grew rapidly. The Peabody name became well known around Chicago as a source for coal and sales increased dramatically to homes and small businesses.

By the late 1880s Peabody was able to buy out his partner. In 1890 his company was incorporated in Illinois as the Peabody Coal Company. Just five years later, Peabody Coal opened its first mine (Mine No. 1) in Williamson County in southern Illinois. By controlling its own mine, Peabody mapped a trail many coal producers would follow. Instead of merely supplying coal to homes and businesses, his company mined and then sold its own coal. Eventually, producing coal became more lucrative than selling. So began a long history of mining for Peabody, whose rise to prominence was a sign of the times.

In the late 1800s and early 1900s, coal had a myriad of uses. It was burned in fireplaces to provide heat for homes and businesses. It was burned in steam engines to provide power for the railroad and shipping industries. Even when diesel fuel pushed steam engines to the back burner, the increasingly widespread use of electricity brought coal to even more prominence. As electricity spread to homes and businesses, utility plants began to clamor for coal in order to produce enough power to meet the demands of this new market. In 1903, Peabody Coal signed a long-term contract with a major electric utility — thereby establishing a benchmark deal for mining operations that would be replicated with coal removed from Quail Lakes.

By 1949 Peabody Coal was listed on the New York Stock Exchange and by the mid-1950s Peabody ranked eighth in the nation among coal producers. But problems loomed for Peabody, which began to lose market share due partly to its reliance on more costly underground mines. Surface mining was growing in popularity because it yielded more coal and was less expensive. After suffering heavy losses in the 1950s, Peabody merged with the larger Sinclair Coal Company in 1955. The merger was a success. Peabody (the name was retained after the merger due to its listing on the NYSE) doubled production and sales. By 1968, when Kennecott Copper Corporation acquired it, Peabody was the largest coal producer in the United States.

Problems arose again, however, when the Federal Trade Commission ruled that Kennecott's purchase of Peabody violated The Clayton Antitrust Act of 1914. While Kennecott challenged the ruling, Peabody began shedding some holdings — including, eventually, the land that would become Quail Lakes.

All this is quite interesting for me since Peabody Energy is today an important customer for Caterpillar. Diane and I are also happy to call Peabody CEO Greg Boyce and his wife Lisa good friends.

While Peabody battled legal difficulties, a new player emerged on the central Illinois coal stage. That was ASARCO, which traced its history back to 1899 and to an organization then known as the American Smelting and Refining Company that was founded by Henry Huttleston Rogers. Rogers was a famed capitalist, industrialist, and financier who formed the Standard Oil Company trust and was ranked No. 22 all-time in terms of overall wealth in U.S. history according to *The Wealthy 100: From Benjamin Franklin to Bill Gates — A Ranking of the Richest Americans, Past and Present*. Rogers worked with partners to start ASARCO under New Jersey laws, which were at the time more favor-

Doug Oberhelman

able to setting up companies that would not be deemed monopolies.

At the same time, the Guggenheim family was heavily involved in smelting operations in the western United States and Mexico. The Guggenheims saw ASARCO as a threat and eventually took control of the company by acquiring 50 percent of its stock. From there ASARCO continued to grow, changing names slightly from time to time and eventually spreading into coal mining in central Illinois under a division it called the Midland Coal Company.

That brings us back to Peoria County and to our property, Quail Lakes. Surface mining in Peoria County started slowly in 1928 with a few thousand tons mined per year from above-ground operations. No major mining was done until 1951, when production soared to 150,136 tons. From there, coal tonnage taken from surface mines would only increase thanks mainly to Midland Coal Company.

Peabody started mining what it called the Elm Mine in 1968 and set up headquarters four miles east of Quail Lakes. But on Nov. 25, 1970, ASARCO spent $24 million to purchase four Illinois coal mines from Peabody. The mines had aggregate capacity of about 6 million tons per year. Selling the mines allowed Peabody — then a subsidiary of Kennecott Copper Corp. — to divest itself of the properties and to come into compliance with a 1967 federal court judgment. Included in the sale were vast acres of potential coal-mining ground in Peoria, Knox, Fulton, and Stark counties. Over the next two decades Midland extensively mined that land.

Those mines operated during the boom time of Illinois surface mining. In 1947, Illinois had 39 surface mines and 120 underground mines and employed 31,400 workers according to the *Coal Report of Illinois*. By 1968, almost 60 percent of the coal mined in Illinois came from surface mines. And from 1965-70, production from above-ground mines topped that of underground mines in Illinois. From 1962-78, surface mining impacted 98,000 acres — while all the acres surface mined in the 100 years before that totaled 103,000.

Several factors contributed to the boom. For one thing, companies were able to mine coal on the surface with fewer workers. Being less labor-intensive was a plus. Then too, surface mining was more productive than underground mining and was safer. In 2008, non-fatal mine accidents for underground miners was 4.6 per 100 workers compared to

1.5 per 100 workers for surface mining, according to the IDCEO. Less costly. More efficient. Safer. The decision to pursue surface mining was an easy one for most operators.

That decision was made even easier by technological advances that made it faster and easier for mine operators to reach the coal. It's much easier to utilize bigger machines in a surface-mining situation, since machinery and workers are not encumbered by overhead restrictions. The differences were dramatic. From tiny, one-yard dipper capacities, shovels grew to handle much, much more overburden.

One of the dominant players in the world of surface-mining equipment was the Marion Steam Shovel Company, founded in 1884 in Marion, Ohio. Marion made its name with a stronger bucket design that allowed for larger loads. Marion shovels set numerous earthmoving records in the early 1900s and played a role in building the Panama Canal. In 1915 Marion introduced the world's first electric-powered

Marion Power Shovel Company's famed The Captain moves overburden at a mine in southern Illinois. This monster shovel had a 180-cubic-yard dipper and stood 21 stories tall when it worked in the coal mines from 1965-91. Photo courtesy of Caterpillar Inc. Corporate Archives.

stripping shovel, the Model 271 that weighed in at 293 tons and had a five-yard bucket. Electric power became the standard for stripping shovels by the mid-1920s. As steam power became less popular, Marion changed its name to the Marion Power Shovel Company.

Through the 1920s and 30s, Marion prospered thanks largely to rising demand for surface mining and road building. Marion shovels also helped build the Hoover Dam and New York City's Holland Tunnel. As more coal-fired power plants were built in the 1950s, demand for coal boomed and equipment makers responded. In 1956 Marion built its first Model 5760 for the Hanna Coal Company in eastern Ohio. The 5760 had a 65-cubic-yard dipper, a 150-foot boom and could handle up to 100-foot walls of soil and rock. This new machine was called "The Mountaineer" and started a virtual arms race between shovel builders, who worked to create ever-larger machines.

Marion's quest culminated in its famed 6360. Called The Captain, this massive machine worked for Southwestern Illinois Coal Corp. at its Captain Mine in Perry County near Percy, Illinois. I remember hearing about The Captain from people all the time while working as a district manager for Caterpillar. This shovel was that famous. The 6360 had a 180-cubic-yard dipper, stood 21 stories tall and weighed 28 million pounds — which at the time was a record for the heaviest mobile land machine ever built.

The Captain cost a reported $15 million and worked from 1965-91 when a hydraulic leak caused a fire that burned an electric panel and rendered the shovel unusable. The Captain was then sold for scrap metal. Marion built three more huge shovels after that, but the 5900 it built in 1971 — with a 105-cubic-yard bucket — was the last stripping shovel built by any manufacturer.

Marion's competitor in the quest to build "The Largest Machine to Walk the Earth" was Bucyrus International, Inc. Bucyrus' rise to surface mining prominence began in 1880 when Ohio business magnate Daniel P. Eells and a group of six other investors from Cleveland purchased the Bucyrus Machine Company of Bucyrus, Ohio. Eels and his associates renamed the business the Bucyrus Foundry and Manufacturing Company and started producing handcars, locomotive drive wheels, and other components for the railroad industry.

That changed dramatically when the Ohio Central Railroad and

Quail Lakes & Coal

Big Muskie dwarfs other mining equipment. Built by Bucyrus International, Big Muskie was the largest dragline ever made and was as wide an eight-lane highway. Its bucket weighed 230 tons when empty and had a capacity of 220 cubic yards. Photo courtesy of Caterpillar Inc. Corporate Archives.

Northern Pacific Railroad ordered steam shovels in 1882. A light bulb went on in corporate headquarters. By 1898, Bucyrus had an annual output of 24 steam shovels. In the spring of 1893 the company began operations in South Milwaukee, and that summer incorporated as The Bucyrus Steam Shovel and Dredge Company of Wisconsin.

After reorganizing in the 1890s, Bucyrus further established its place in the market by increasing production and unveiling a steady stream of innovations. In 1911, Bucyrus unveiled its first dragline machines with tank-tread-style crawlers. Bucyrus also played a huge role in Panama Canal construction and is credited for most of the earth and rock moving during the peak of canal construction. President Theodore Roosevelt even posed for photographs on a Bucyrus machine when he visited the Panama Canal construction site.

From there Bucyrus went on to acquire several smaller companies, including the Erie Steam Shovel Company in 1927, which was then the

Doug Oberhelman

largest producer of small excavating machines. The new Bucyrus-Erie Company moved into the top position among small shovel producers. In 1935 Bucyrus-Erie produced the 1,250-ton 950B, the first shovel propelled by electric motors placed at the crawlers. Prior to that, power had been transmitted from motors in the upper works through various gear trains, chains, and shafts. Using a motor at each crawler assembly was easier and quickly became the industry standard. Even so, the motors were not designed for speed, as most stripping shovels traveled at 0.25 miles per hour or less.

But it was in the world of draglines that Bucyrus had its biggest impact — eventually making history with Big Muskie, the largest dragline ever built. Big Muskie took several years to build at a reported cost of $25 million. The machine stood 20 stories tall, was as wide as an eight-lane highway, weighed 27 million pounds, and was powered by ten 1,250-horsepower motors. Big Muskie's bucket weighed 230 tons when empty and had a capacity of 220 cubic yards. The boom was 310 feet long. Big Muskie worked at the Muskingum Mine near Cumberland, Ohio, for the Central Ohio Coal Company from 1969-91 and used 13,800 volts of electricity via a trailing cable — the equivalent power needed to light 27,500 homes. After it was removed from service in 1991, Big Muskie sat for eight years before it was sold for scrap for $700,000. No larger dragline has been built since.

In 1997, Bucyrus acquired its longtime rival, the Marion Power Shovel Company. The Marion plant in Ohio was closed and operations were moved to Bucyrus' plant in South Milwaukee. And in July of 2011 Caterpillar proudly acquired Bucyrus — a purchase that further strengthened Caterpillar's role in the mining industry. That acquisition is part of a long history at Caterpillar of helping partners in the mining industry by improving the equipment and service we provide — whether that's a bulldozer, loader, scraper, excavator, truck, or now even a shovel, dragline or drill.

In the last chapter, we mentioned Caterpillar had its roots in agricultural equipment, and Caterpillar was still building "ag" tractors when the Holt family moved its business to open a factory in East Peoria in 1910. At the time, Pliny Holt — nephew of Benjamin Holt — wrote, "I am sure that this ... marks the beginning of one of the largest enterprises in the Middle West, and assures the City of Peoria of an industry that they

Quail Lakes & Coal

Here is a Caterpillar D8H at work in 1965 at a coal mine. Photo courtesy of Caterpillar Inc. Corporate Archives.

will be proud of in the future." How prescient those words proved to be. But track-type tractors were soon used for much more than farming and Benjamin Holt was one of the first to recognize the capabilities of his machines.

In World War I, Holt's Caterpillar tractors helped haul artillery and supplies overseas. Back on U.S. soil, those same tractors were used to build and grade roads, to haul equipment and to help anywhere people needed reliable, versatile machines. Naturally, that included work in the mining industry. But first, in April of 1925, a new company was formed under the name Caterpillar Tractor Co. The C.L. Best Tractor Co. (founded by Daniel Best's son C.L. Best) and the Holt Manufacturing Company were merged into this new Caterpillar company. In the years since, Caterpillar's busy engineers have never stopped looking for ways to make earthmoving and mining easier.

One of the real workhorses of the mining industry rolled off the lines in East Peoria in 1935 when the RD8 Tractor made its debut. You may better recognize the machine as the D8, since Caterpillar later dropped the "R" from the name. The D8 and its 1955 successor the D9 were soon ubiquitous in mining operations all over Illinois, the U.S. and the world.

Many more innovations came after World War II. In 1946 Caterpillar introduced its first track-type, tractor-towed scrapers (the No. 60, No. 70, and No. 80). Wheeled tractor scrapers got their start in 1941 with the DW10 Tractor, but production was suspended from 1943-45. In 1947 Caterpillar released the No. 10 Scraper and an updated version of the DW10. By 1948, Caterpillar introduced a 15 cubic-yard DW21 with a No. 21 Scraper that was the company's first integrated/self-propelled wheel tractor-scraper. Production of the DW21 started in 1951. In 1952, the company debuted the No. 6 Shovel, its first track loader and the first track loader with an integrated design. Caterpillar engineers combined a front-end loader attachment with a track-type tractor to create this integrated design. The slick machine had immediate uses for loading coal in mines all over the country. A few years later in 1959 Caterpillar came out with our first wheel loader, the No. 944 "Wheel-type Traxcavator." Today, with more than a dozen different wheel-loader models, Caterpillar has the world's most comprehensive line.

In 1962 Caterpillar released its first off-highway truck, the 769. Designed for long, hard use, the 769 had non-fade braking with oil-cooled disc brakes and other features designed to help operators. From there the company made changes in trucks — quickly and steadily, responding to the mining industry's demand for larger equipment capable of moving more material. Most of these trucks were built in Decatur, Illinois, just across town from Millikin University where I went to college. Capacities soared from 35 tons with the 769 to the 50-ton 773 in 1970, then to the 85-ton 777 in 1974. Today, Caterpillar produces mining trucks like the 797F that can haul up to 400 tons at a time.

And so it goes. The improvements in technology have helped make mining more effective and more efficient. No wonder surface mining soared in importance.

At the start of the 1970s, The Illinois Basin was producing 140 million tons per year, or roughly 24 percent of all the coal mined in the U.S. Almost 60 percent of that coal came from surface mines. However, the expansion of surface mining was not without vocal critics, particularly in central Illinois where much of the ground mined was "prime" farmland. Losing fertile farmland angered farmers and worried even conservative Republican politicians like Senator Everett Dirksen of Pekin. In the 1940s, Dirksen introduced federal legislation requiring coal companies to reclaim land after they were finished mining. While Dirksen's bill did not advance beyond subcommittee, his ideas marked the start of what in the 1970s became a heated Congressional battle. Reclamation was one issue, but so was concern about acid rain and the emissions of high-sulfur coal like that mined in Illinois.

It was against that backdrop that Quail Lakes joined the list of active Illinois coal mines in 1976.

Doug Oberhelman

CHAPTER THREE
MINING AT QUAIL LAKES

Folks in the quiet town of Elmwood — where the population is 2,100 and the stoplight count is zero — remember the days when huge steel dinosaurs walked ponderously through the area. Seeing massive mining machines lurching across the landscape has a way of sticking in the mind. And from the 1960s into the 1980s, those monster machines were a part of life for residents of Elmwood and many other towns in central Illinois.

My friend Bill Atwood, who is our property manager at Quail Lakes, came to the Elmwood area in 1970. He has vivid memories of the big mining machines. "It was very impressive. I'd be out there hauling rock and here's this great big truck that looks as big as a building coming past me," Atwood recalled. "To me the shovel was the most impressive. It was huge."

What made the experience even more memorable for locals was that you couldn't see a stripping shovel in action just anywhere. These monster machines were pretty much limited to open-pit mines. "For a guy out of Wisconsin who had never seen anything bigger than a [semi-truck] it was pretty impressive," marveled Jim Grimm, who worked for Midland Coal Company in various roles at the Elm Mine.

And from 1930 to the 1980s, west-central Illinois was one of the booming areas for surface mines in Illinois and the United States. During those years mining was a way of life in Fulton, Knox, Stark, and — eventually — Peoria counties. Mike Kepple grew up in Fulton County in the 1950s and 60s and has vivid memories of the days when Midland Coal was mining around Middle Grove, Consolidation Coal Company had an operation near Norris, and both the Freeman United Coal Mining Company and Peabody Coal Company were active around Canton. "Fulton County was the biggest strip-mine county in the state at that time," Kepple stressed. "In Fulton County you were a farmer, you worked at International Harvester or you worked in the coal mines. That was it."

Doug Oberhelman

The story was similar in Knox County from 1956 to the 1980s and, to a lesser degree, in southwest Peoria County where Midland Coal ran the show from 1968 to 1984. "At one time we had Elm, Edwards, Allendale, and Mecco mines all running at the same time and we had an office out there with probably 20 people in just our accounting department to support all the mines," Grimm said. "There was always a mine opening or closing."

The Elm Mine, which eventually included Quail Lakes, opened in 1968. By the time workers loaded the last rail car with coal at the tipple near Trivoli, Elm Mine and Midland's other surface-mining operation out of Edwards encompassed more than 50,000 acres in Peoria County. The dividing line for the two surface mines was Eden Road, with the Edwards Mine to the east and Elm Mine to the west. Operations ceased in 1984 at Quail Lakes, which was the last site Midland mined in Peoria County.

All coal from the Elm Mine was shipped by rail car to a Wisconsin Power and Light power plant in Sheboygan, Wisconsin. Coincidentally, that plant is not very far from Ripon, Wisconsin — where Diane's great grandfather Robert Allen settled in the early 1800s after arriving from England. Robert Allen, born in 1822, raised his family in Ripon, including Diane's grandfather Frederick William Allen and her father, Fred Allen. The family still owns the original farmhouse and we make trips back there each summer, though we have recently added an air conditioner in case it gets too hot.

Diane's grandfather was a market hunter in the late 1800s before he became police chief in Ripon. Being a market hunter means he made his living off wild game. So he would take brass shells and shoot 500 birds at a time and then take them to Milwaukee to sell for 25 cents each. Sometimes he would get so tired he would load powder and shell in the wrong order in his gun!

The last Midland mine to open in Peoria County was at Quail Lakes in 1976, a year when production of the Elm Mine stood at 716,653 tons. Before mining started, workers first had to move heavy equipment into the area. Bulldozers, scrapers, and loaders were impressive enough and drew considerable interest from the numerous Caterpillar employees in the area who had helped design and build those machines. Elmwood is located just 35 minutes from several Caterpillar plants and, as in many

Frederick William Allen (far left) and his buddies pose with ducks they shot while hunting for market in the 1800s in Wisconsin. Frederick is Diane's grandfather and grew up in Ripon, Wisconsin, not far from where coal from Quail Lakes was later used to generate electricity.

Illinois communities, a sizable number of workers make a daily commute to our offices or plants. But the real memorable monsters as mining started at Quail Lakes were the Marion 5761 shovel and a German-made Kolbe bucket-wheel excavator that came from United Electric Coal Companies in 1970 after a career working at mines in Fulton County. These were truly huge machines.

The Marion shovel — one of 16 of the 5761 model made by Marion from 1959 to 1970 — weighed more than 3,700 tons. *In Giant Earth-Moving Equipment*, author Eric C. Orlemann described the 5761 as, "The most popular model line of super-stripping shovels produced by any manufacturer." When it debuted in 1959 the 5761 was the world's largest stripping shovel, with a dipper capacity of 65 cubic yards and a 170-foot boom. Eight crawler assemblies moved the huge shovel and each section stood 8 feet tall, 23 feet long, and 5 feet wide.

Grimm came to Illinois from Mineral Point, Wisconsin, and hired on with ASARCO after graduating from the University of Wisconsin with a degree in mining engineering. After first dreaming of working in a western copper mine, Grimm settled on a Midwestern coal mine. "I didn't even know they had coal in Illinois," he joked. But Grimm soon learned that coal mining was a big part of the Illinois economy. So did his family. Whenever relatives came south to visit, Grimm made sure to give tours of the big 5761 shovel. His Wisconsin clan was always impressed by the machine. "They just loved those tours. Nobody sees machinery that big. And nobody can fathom how big it is until they are on it," Grimm noted, his eyes dancing at the memory.

The huge Kolbe was more than 400 feet long, weighed 2,100 tons and stood 150 feet tall. A similar machine used in Fulton County was built on the lower works of a retired Marion 5600 stripping shovel from 1929, according to Keith Haddock's *The Earthmover Encyclopedia*. The digging wheel was 27 feet in diameter and could move up to 2 million cubic yards of overburden per month. Operators were perched 90 feet in the air.

Both the shovel and the wheel excavator came to the Elmwood area from Middle Grove, a town in Fulton County that is surrounded by older surface-mine lakes. Mining there ceased in 1968 and Peabody workers moved the heavy equipment about 10 miles east to Elmwood in a slow, dinosaur-like procession. Moving a machine as heavy as the 5761 was laborious, and involved the use of large wooden "mats" for the shovel and wheel to crawl across. In the case of the Elm Mine, mats were made of railroad ties banded together. "The machine would walk so far, swing around, hook up one of the mats [it had crawled across] with its bucket, swing back around, drop it down and then walk some more," Grimm explained.

Even so, things didn't always go as planned. Whenever possible, the machines would walk on haul roads used to move coal from the pit to the tipple, the structure where coal was loaded into railroad cars. But that was not always possible, particularly in new mining areas. Ken Miars worked in the Elm Mine and at other sites for 26 years in various jobs. He remembered a few incidents vividly. In one case the shovel had to move across Illinois State Route 78. That required workers to amass 12-foot piles of dirt over the blacktop to prevent damage from the massive machine. And because it was crossing from the jurisdiction of one union to that of another, crews running the machine had to change

Quail Lakes & Coal

A Marion 5761 shovel stands tall in a deep surface-mine pit. This is the same model of Marion shovel that was used during the mining at Quail Lakes. Photo courtesy of Caterpillar Inc. Corporate Archives.

midway across the road.

That was nothing compared to the problem encountered one day while the 5761 shovel moved toward a surface mine located a few miles east of Quail Lakes. Partway to its destination, the shovel had to cross an agricultural field about two miles east of Quail Lakes. "I'll never forget that," Miars recalled with a shake of his head. "The shovel went out of sight and was buried. It was a mess. They didn't anticipate the ground being that soft but it was. When you bury a shovel it is very time-consuming. It took three or four weeks of work to get that out." Workers had to use two tiers of mats for the shovel to gain traction and ultimately pull itself out of the deep, soft hole. Driving past the site some 30 years later, corn stands tall. "But if you dig down about 10 feet in there I bet you'd find mats of railroad ties," Miars chuckled.

"The best quote was some old farmer came out afterwards and said, 'I could have told you that was a wet spot, boys,' " recounted Phil Christy, a land reclamation specialist for Midland Coal. "They had to dig that thing out and that mess was there for years."

Once mining was ready to start at Quail Lakes, both the shovel and the wheel moved into position on the north end of the property. The machines began digging near where we now have a shed to keep our Caterpillar machines that we use to make improvements at Quail Lakes. As active mining started in 1976, the wheel and shovel operated simultaneously. At that time, the Quail Lakes property was mostly agricultural land with some timber along the small tributary of Kickapoo Creek that ran through the property. There were a few homes, some outbuildings, a barn or two, and at least one fish-filled farm pond.

The rock and soil overburden at that end was not particularly deep and mining started quickly at first. "It was so shallow there you could jump off the high wall," Miars said. But not all was smooth stripping. That was due in large part to the hard work of Avery Dalton and his descendants some 100 years earlier. Dalton, you may recall, spent time digging for coal in the area he called Lost Prairie. That's the same general area where surface mining of Quail Lakes began.

"I know we opened it up with the shovel and we ran into problems with lots of old works over there. There were tunnels from underground mining," Grimm said. "The shovel would lift what shale there was and it was shallow on that north end, maybe just 20 feet deep. He'd lift that material off and sometimes they had to use mats because you could literally see the drifts and stuff in there. [The tunnels] would be 4-5 feet wide and full of water. And it really made it very difficult as far as stripping in there with that shovel. The worst thing that could happen is one of your crawlers on your machines falling into [the old mine tunnels]. Because they are only 30-40 feet deep it slows you up. You just couldn't move through the field like you wanted to."

Because the shovel and wheel both sit on the coal seam, they had problems when a seam of coal had been removed. Operators would have to scoop up shale to fill the cavity before they could move the machine. And then workers would have to separate the rock and shale from

Quail Lakes & Coal

A Bucyrus-Erie 2560 dragline rips through overburden at the Elm Mine on or near Quail Lakes. This dragline was built four miles east of Quail Lakes after parts were hauled in on railroad cars. Photo courtesy of Phil Christy.

Four smiling miners pose inside the dragline from the Elm Mine's Bucyrus-Erie 2560 dragline. This bucket had a capacity of 85 cubic yards. Photo courtesy of Phil Christy.

the coal as they loaded coal haulers. That was not an uncommon problem for surface mines, according to Grimm. Old works were common in areas where the coal seam was exposed. As we learned from the days of the earliest settlers, coal has always been a valued commodity. Yet it's ironic to think mines that helped warm Avery Dalton's family later caused some of his descendants — or at least descendants of his friends and neighbors — to grumble as they had a day's work delayed by the collapse of a 100-year-old shaft.

Miars was working the night the Marion shovel dug into one of those old works, a shaft located on the northeast corner of Quail Lakes. "We hit that baby and the water puked out of there and just literally drowned the pit we were in. The water came clear up to the top of the crawlers. I was on duty that night and it was third shift when we hit it. The guys called me and said, 'We've got a problem here,'" Miars recalled. "Well, we set up pumps and tried to get the water out. That took awhile. Once we got the water out, me and a couple other guys took a lantern in there and walked in about 50 or 60 feet. It was just an old underground mine. And it was stinking in there. We found an old cart and some shovels and a pick. I was about half scared to go in there, anyway. I didn't know what the hell was going to happen. So we just left the old coal cart and picks down there and said, 'Let's get the hell out.' You just don't know what is going to happen. Eventually we just blocked it off with the shovel. That was the end of the pit, anyway. So after we got the water out we went back to stripping."

Today all that marks that spot is a row of willow trees. Until this book project, I had no idea what was located under those willows. But that same location is the spot where Diane and I shot our first covey of quail on Quail Lakes. That was back in 2008 and we were hunting a hillside above there. Then we came down to the willows and, boom, the quail flushed. To think there's a mine shaft under the same spot is just one more illustration of the healing power of time. It's astonishing to think those monster machines were on this property less than 30 years ago and had it torn open at least 75 feet deep. But today there's no sign of that mining. Instead there are quail and other wildlife using the land. Amazing.

But those big machines were here. And working with a machine as large and powerful as a huge Marion shovel was memorable. Richard

Quail Lakes & Coal

Coal sits waiting to be shipped outside the tipple of the Elm Mine near Trivoli, Illinois. Coal from Quail Lakes was processed in this tipple before being shipped to Sheboygan, Wisconsin. Photo courtesy of Phil Christy.

Coon of Elmwood spent parts of four years working in surface mines in Knox County. Among his tasks was checking the time clock on a Marion 5760 shovel, which was comparable to the newer 5761 used at Quail Lakes. Coon's job required daily trips into the coal pit, which in and of itself was memorable. "You're really tiny down there when you've got 60 foot [or more] of overburden on this side, the big slag pile on this side where they are digging the coal out, you've got the huge stripper, you've got haulage trucks going back and forth, and you've got the coal loader down there," Coon said. The shovel was most impressive of all, though. "It was the hugest machine I'll probably ever be in."

Coon's daily trips required him to walk under the shovel as it was working. Once there, he would pull himself up on a ladder in the middle of the huge machine. After ascending three rungs, he would come to a platform. Then he walked into a two-person, electric elevator. "You get in that, push the button and go up to the second floor. The first thing you hear when it opens is this huge whining of gears and motors," Coon recalled. "After you get out on that floor, the cables are continually lowering the bucket and picking up the bucket." Operators could choose between two cubicles located on either side of the machine. Coon would walk to the time clock on the back wall and remove a paper disk that recorded each swing of the shovel's boom. "The mine wanted to know how many swings each operator was doing during his shift," Coon explained.

At Quail Lakes, the Kolbe wheel was eventually sidelined, giving way to the Marion shovel. Towards the end of the mining process as the pits became deeper, the shovel was joined by a Bucyrus-Erie 2560 dragline. The dragline was built in 1967 on a property four miles east of the mine. Construction took one year. "They shipped everything in by rail. There was a spur brought out from Farmington and Middle Grove that was built right into the mine site," Grimm recalled.

When completed, the dragline sat on a 65-foot tub that had ground pressure of just 17 psi. "That's less pressure than your wife's high heels," Christy said admiringly. No mats were needed to move the dragline into position, as it had "walking feet" on which it moved.

The dragline bucket had a capacity of 85 cubic yards and mine operators were eager to get that big bucket into action. "We felt the dragline was a more efficient stripping machine than the shovel or wheel," Grimm said. Interestingly, a similar shift in machinery was being seen in coal mining across the country. John W. Page first invented draglines in 1904 for use in digging the Chicago Drainage Canal. Because of their greater boom length, draglines were better suited to pile overburden farther away from the working area. Shovels, however, had to pile overburden closer to the pit. This could create problems when spoil piles slid back into the mining area.

Over time as mines went deeper for coal, mine managers increasingly turned to the dragline. As Eric Orlemann noted in his *Power Shovels: The World's Mightiest Mining and Construction Excavators*: "It seems the end of the super-stripping shovel ended as fast as it began. Though these magnificent shovels were the best of their breed, the mining industry ultimately chose the walking dragline as the preferred method of reaching deeply buried coal seams. Even though the shovel and dragline had been allies over the decades, in many instances working side by side in mining operations across the United States, the greater working range of the dragline would ultimately prove too much for the shovel to overcome."

The goal was to move as much overburden as fast as possible to make mining more profitable. The same pattern emerged at Quail Lakes. The shovel and wheel opened the mine and started on the areas with less overburden. But as the pits got deeper and the loads got larger, mine operators walked the dragline into place. Grimm said that for the final several years at Quail Lakes both the shovel and dragline operated simultaneously in a two-pit operation.

At Quail Lakes, all three monster machines worked to uncover a No. 6 seam of coal that averaged 42 inches in thickness and ranged from 40-75 feet below the surface. "I remember that [coal] recovery was about

The Kolbe bucket-wheel excavator and the Marion 5761 shovel move overburden in this shot of a pit at Quail Lakes in the late 1970s. A smaller P&H coal loader is also shown in the picture. Photo courtesy of Phil Christy.

60 percent of the seam by the time you cleaned it," Grimm explained. He estimated the mine averaged 50,000 tons of coal per month. Once the shovel, wheel or dragline exposed the coal seam, loaders moved in to scoop the coal into trucks — or coal haulers as they were called. At the Elm Mine, workers relied mostly on P&H loaders with 16-yard buckets that had been brought east from ASARCO's western copper mines. Coal haulers were typically Dart 120-ton trucks. Once the coal haulers were full, they headed out of the pit, got onto the haulage road and went to the tipple, the place where coal is washed and readied for shipping.

The tipple for the Elm Mine was located north of Trivoli, four miles east of Quail Lakes. Haul trucks brought coal to a hopper. At the bottom of the hopper was a conveyor with feeders that moved coal into the processing plant. Inside the large building, coal was sorted, cleaned, and sized to a uniform product that ranged between 4/100 inches to 1¼ inches in diameter. The first step in preparation was to remove rock and clay (called gob) from the coal. Grimm said separation was achieved using centrifuges and tanks of pulsating water. Because coal is softer, it can be crushed and freed from rock. Coal's lower specific gravity also means it "floats" in agitated water while heavier materials such as rock sink. The final step was to remove the slurry — finer coal, clay, and sand that could be washed away.

All this was done to make the coal ready for combustion in steam boilers at Wisconsin Power and Light's plant in Sheboygan. All coal mined at Quail Lakes was shipped by train to the Wisconsin power plant 280 miles away. Once coal was sorted, cleaned, and sized, it was carried out of the tipple by conveyors to a stockpile. Feeders would then load railroad cars that reached the tipple via a railroad spur. Every three days or so, mine workers would load a 100-car train to head north to Wisconsin. "We'd put a couple of dozers on the job to push coal into feeders to feed the train," Miars recalled. "It would take one whole day to load the unit train." By the end of the contract with Wisconsin Power and Light, coal from Quail Lakes was selling for $39 per ton.

Other machinery on site included several older Cat D8 and D9 bulldozers that had been built just 35 minutes away in East Peoria. The mine also used several Caterpillar 631 scrapers and a few Peoria-built WABCO scrapers, several WABCO dump trucks, and a Bucyrus-Erie vertical drill with a 12-inch bore. The Elm Mine also had a unique water truck with a 10,000-gallon tank built onto the frame of a Cat 631 scraper. We'll talk more about that later.

In its heyday, there were approximately 160 workers employed at the Elm Mine according to Christy. Coincidentally, Christy is the same person we negotiated with to purchase Quail Lakes. He is a very knowledgeable guy and seems to know every piece of territory in three counties. Out of the 160 employees, Grimm said probably 120-130 were union workers and 30-40 were company workers. Work was underway 24 hours a day, seven days a week. "There may have been a day when, if you had a pit full of coal, you'd give them a Sunday off," Grimm recalled. "But it was generally seven days a week."

Jobs were varied. Operators of the shovel, wheel, and dragline had the glamor spots. But there were also mechanics. Electricians. Civil engineers. Truck drivers. Heavy equipment operators. All had a place in the mine. Dragline and shovel crews were made up of four people by union rule. There were three workers on the wheel at any given time. Two loaders were running in each pit most of the time along with as many as a dozen bulldozers and six or seven coal haulers. "We loaded coal on day shift only. Once in awhile we'd load on second shift, but they didn't like to unless we had to," Miars noted. "The reason you had to was because maybe the shovel was sitting there waiting for an open pit to strip. If the machine was on top of you, you loaded the coal and got it ready to go."

Miars was one who appreciated the career opportunities mining provided. In addition to working as a pit boss, pit foreman, blasting foreman, and timekeeper, Miars also worked as a reclamation foreman at Quail Lakes. He liked mining because by working third shift (midnight to 8 a.m.) he still had time to officiate sporting events. "As far as strip mining goes, I made good money. It was a $60,000 a year job, no doubt about it. I put two kids through college with my job. And [the company] helped my daughter. She had congenital hip problems and they took care of her. Thank God for the coal company."

Not everyone shared that emotion. Grimm joked that he did his grocery shopping out of town so he wouldn't run into anyone who wanted to complain about mining. One of the most contentious issues was the blasting of shale. Blast crews worked during the day to loosen shale so the shovel or dragline could more easily move the overburden. Blasting was done horizontally in the sidewalls of the shovel pit using 300 to 400 pounds of ammonium nitrate. In the dragline pit, blast crews drilled vertically. All blasting had to be done at least 100 feet from the highway, though Miars recalled one occasion when Illinois Route 78 had to be closed because it was covered with shale from a large explosion. To keep the peace with neighbors, Grimm would often visit during blasting. "It didn't cost us anything, it was just good PR," Grimm concluded.

The pit was a unique setting that looked somewhat like a moonscape, since it was littered with rocks and black coal and large machinery. At Quail Lakes, the deepest pits were about 75 feet down and typically 100 feet wide, leaving high sides towering over the workers. The elements had a major impact. Snow created problems, but ice was worse, since it coated machines and roads and slowed the mining process. Rain was the worst, though. "Rain screwed you up worse than anything. Rain in a strip mine is a no-no. It's just the opposite of the farmer. The drier it was the better we liked it," Miars said.

"If it never rained in my 23 years [of mining] that would have been great," Grimm agreed. "I'd take the cold any day. I hated the rain because rain made mud."

Rain also created worse problems. If workers knew a rainstorm was brewing, they would often pull machinery up onto high ground to keep the motors and cabs from being swamped. Pumps were also running all the time to keep pits dry. Workers built terraces, dams, and other water-control structures on high walls to divert water from the pit. Even so, plans sometimes failed or storms brewed up unexpectedly. Those were not happy days at the Elm Mine. "We had many times where the loader cabs, which are 15-20 feet above the ground, were under water. They would be totally flooded," Grimm grumbled. "Then things would come to a stop. You'd pull all the motors off things and send them away to be cleaned and baked again and life went on."

Even without adverse weather, life in the pit was hectic. "It was wild down there. You had machines running, haul trucks driving, water trucks, loaders, blasting going on," marveled Miars. "It was wild."

But it was organized chaos, according to Grimm. Every worker had a job to do and so long as people did their jobs, mining moved forward steadily. "With the shovel you had to get the coal out in order for the shovel to keep digging and to give it somewhere to dump," Grimm said.

"The same with the dragline. If you didn't get the coal, you didn't have a place to dig."

Up above the pit, Cat 631 scrapers ran constantly on first and second shifts to move topsoil to locations where it was stockpiled for later use in reclamation. Third shift was often a time for overhauling equipment. "Your biggest maintenance on the dragline was your drag cables and your hoist cables. They take a lot of abuse," Miars explained. "And on the shovel, the teeth of the shovel would take most of the brunt of the digging."

Occasionally there were fringe benefits to the mining process. In the case of Quail Lakes, the property included a small one-acre lake in the path of the dragline in the southern part of the property. "We got to it and drained it before the dragline got to it," Grimm recalled. "There were big bass and lots of catfish in there and our guys after work would go in with chest waders in the mud to try to catch these fish. I can remember Bob "Bolly" Chambers with mud up to his waist and gunny sacks that he was throwing the fish into."

Grimm also salvaged wood from an old barn on the property that had been built with mortise and tenon, an old form of wood construction that involves inserting a tenon at the end of one board into a mortise hole cut into another board. Though very basic, mortise-and-tenon joints are also very strong. "There was not a nail in that thing and it was well-built," Grimm marveled. The Dalton family may have constructed the barn, as they had a reputation for barn building. Interestingly enough, descendants of Avery Dalton are still involved in construction around Elmwood as part of Jeremy Dalton's company, Dalton Construction.

There were also benefits to township road commissioners in exchange for letting the mine company close roads. "You had to work with the township road commissioners. You had to get their approval to close roads," Grimm recalled. "We would buy them road graders and end loaders and stuff like that for the townships which maybe lost some tax revenues from the ground until the road was back in place." At Quail Lakes a part of Taggart Road was closed for several years while the big machines did their work in the pits. In exchange for closing the road, the mine provided Elmwood Township with a used wheel loader from Michigan. Eventually the township traded that machine for a Cat 920 wheel loader, according to Bill Atwood.

Since Quail Lakes was the last site mined in the Elm Mine, there were several other final-cut lakes in the surrounding area that had already filled with water and were stocked with fish. Mining companies stocked some lakes. But anglers and off-duty miners did most of the fish stocking by hauling their catch from lake to lake. "It was in our plan to stock all the lakes, but usually somebody got the lakes stocked before we could get in there," Christy said. "We used to have a lake at each mine where the public could fish and you were supposed to get a permit."

Policing fishing was seldom done, though, so anglers often came and went as they wanted. That sometimes created conflicts. "People would literally stop and park their vehicle on the side of the road while we were hauling coal and they would go in and go fishing," Miars grumbled. "There we were hauling 180 tons of coal and they would get mad because we'd tell them they couldn't fish. There were certain days they could fish, but it wasn't the days we hauled coal. We didn't have time to be looking for them while we were going down the haul road."

Workers also devised unique methods of saving time, including one that involved the previously mentioned water truck on the Cat scraper body. "We had to keep the haul road watered all the time to keep the dust down and keep the residents happy. Well, the haul road went right out past the restaurant out there [The Roadhouse]," Miars said. "We used to back the water truck back into the lake to fill it up with water. As long as you didn't get the cab and the engine in the water you were OK. Once in awhile we'd get stuck and have to do something in there to pull it out. But mostly it was just a quick way to fill the truck. The only bad thing about it was the rear wheels on the water tank had to be pulled off every two weeks or so to make sure there was no water in them."

The same Roadhouse Restaurant is still going strong and is where Diane and I spent many enjoyable evenings early in our marriage, when we had our "luxurious" fifth-wheel trailer before we had a cabin at Quail Lakes. We'd go out to Quail Lakes to hunt or just to walk the land and would stop there for a meal on the way home. Those are some of the fondest memories we have of our early days together.

By 1984, the coal seam at Quail Lakes had been exhausted. As the operation neared its end, Elm Mine managers negotiated for another parcel directly east of Quail Lakes on the Morrison and Mary Wiley Library

Farm. Things looked promising until Wisconsin Power and Light changed plans. "They wanted to build more coal-fired plants and the only way they could get it done was with low-sulfur coal," Grimm said. "That's when they told us that when the contract was done they didn't want any more coal."

That was a shame, according to Christy. "By the end we were getting $39 per ton [in 1984] and that was a good price. And they had a lot of problems getting that worked up to that price," Christy lamented. "The Elm Mine for a long time was not making money. But in the end it was making money because the price they were getting for coal was much higher. It would have been nice to have had another year or two at that time, because we had a good contract."

The same thing was happening all over Illinois. High-sulfur coal was rapidly falling out of favor as companies saw the writing on the wall for amendments to the Clean Air Act that became law in 1990. Earlier amendments to the Clean Air Act had required reductions of sulfur dioxide emissions nationwide. While installing scrubbers may have helped accomplish this goal, most companies opted instead to switch to low-sulfur coal from Wyoming's Powder River Basin. In many places out west, a relatively shallow layer of overburden covered coal, making it cheaper to mine than deeper Illinois seams.

As a result, the demand for Illinois coal largely disappeared in the early 1990s. The boom days were over in central Illinois and most of the state. Mines closed. Workers scrambled for new jobs. Coal employment in Illinois dropped by 62 percent from 1990 to 2008 according to the Department of Commerce and Economic Opportunity.

At the same time, Mother Nature began to work her healing magic on numerous mine properties no longer in use. Trees sprang up around tipples and old mine sheds. Grasses grew. Water filled final-cut lakes. Wild animals began to move back into the mine sites. Corn and beans were planted on reclaimed properties like Quail Lakes. Ironically, the downturn in Illinois surface mining came at a time when reclamation laws had changed dramatically. New federal legislation largely eliminated longstanding concerns over the loss of prime farmland, as we shall see in the next chapter. This also coincided with a growing demand for recreational property and set the stage for the next surface-mine demand cycle that carries on to this day.

Doug Oberhelman

CHAPTER FOUR
WE CAN RECLAIM IT

While riding past Quail Lakes, the former coal miner and reclamation boss Ken Miars of Yates City gestured to fields of corn and beans covering much of the property. "This here," he emphasized by pointing to Quail Lakes, "is $30 per ton coal." Then Miars jerked his thumb toward the hilly, rocky properties across Illinois Route 78. "That over there is $17 per ton coal." To Miars, that's the simple summary of the Surface Mining Control and Reclamation Act of 1977 (SMCRA). In a nutshell, mine reclamation was costly, but effective. "It was good environmentally but it was expensive to the customer," Miars argued. "And it affected everyone who used coal."

Quail Lakes was one of the beneficiaries of the new reclamation law, which passed after years of debate and vetoes in Washington. Once mining ended our property was graded, contoured and managed back into a close approximation of its former self — all thanks to SMCRA. Our friends can't believe the entire property had been "opened" to depths of 75 feet just 35 years ago. That's a positive change, no question. But as with so many things involving energy and the environment, there were tradeoffs too. This is the conundrum of coal. It is relatively inexpensive and abundant and we have increasing demands for energy. But there are consequences to burning coal that we have a responsibility to address.

For the first 100 years of surface mining, the largest changes in the industry came in the form of new machinery. Bigger shovels. Bigger draglines. Bigger bulldozers, scrapers, and haul trucks. But nothing that came before had as large of an impact as the 1977 SMCRA, which in many states halted or at least slowed the spread of surface mines. At the center of the change was economics. Differences between "pre-law" and "post-law" mine land are dramatic. Land mined after SMCRA was required to be restored so that the slope and topography closely resemble its original state. Land also had to be covered with topsoil from the same property that was stockpiled during the mining process.

That meant more work and more expense for mine operators — as much as $10,000 per acre according to Jim Grimm. Yet the extra expense also resulted in a final product that could once again be farmed and that looked, in many cases, very much like the original land. Quail Lakes and other properties across the country are very good examples of "post-law" mining — after which it's almost impossible to tell what actually happened to the land during the mining process.

Establishing federal control over surface mining came only after 40 years of heated discussion in Washington. The move to federal oversight of surface mining gained momentum as the practice became more prevalent after 1930. Losing prime farmland worried some politicians, and the condition of the land after mining worried people who lived in surface-mine country. States began enacting their own laws in the 1930s and 1940s, with Illinois among the leaders by passing its first reclamation law in 1943. While that was voided by the Illinois Supreme Court in 1947 and was never enforced, Illinois later passed several reclamation laws that became policy.

By the time SMCRA was enacted, Illinois was well ahead of the national curve for mine reclamation according to the Illinois Department of Natural Resources' publication, *Citizen's Guide to Coal Mining and Reclamation in Illinois*. That was not really surprising, since Prairie State farmers had grown increasingly worried as farmland was mined for coal. Farmers were and still are a powerful constituency in Illinois and made their voices heard with politicians. In 1940 Senator Everett Dirksen introduced the first federal legislation seeking control of surface mining. Though Dirksen's bill never made it made out of subcommittee, it did add fuel to a dialogue that raged for years in Washington.

The first Illinois law with any teeth was the Open Cut Land Reclamation Act of 1962. This law required mine operators to obtain a permit prior to working the ground and to post a bond to guarantee certain reclamation requirements — hints of what was to come in federal policy. Grading was required to reduce peaks and ridges to a rolling topography on mine sites that were within 600 feet of public roadways and to level the tops of any ridges to a width of at least 440 yards apart. Those ridge tops were then to be seeded or planted.

"It required that if you have this ridge of dirt that's never been touched you had to strike off a pasture, a 12-foot plateau on top of the ridge. Then you had to seed it and get a stand of vegetation to reclaim it," explained Phil Christy, who worked on reclamation for the state of Illinois and for the coal industry. "Then the law in 1968 [the Illinois Surface Mined Land Reclamation Act] upgraded it. It made for a wider strike-off, from 12 to 18 feet. There was also a little more grading and you also had to start covering refuse and gob. You have to place your gob [the waste material left after mining] in a hole and put four feet of dirt on it."

A few years later, environmentally minded Illinois Gov. Richard B. Oglivie signed the 1971 Surface-Mined Land Conservation and Reclamation Act (SMLCRA). This law stipulated some of the toughest restrictions in the country, including a requirement that operators make public filings of reclamation plans with a county clerk according to the *Citizen's Guide to Coal Mining and Reclamation in Illinois*. There was also a waiting period and a provision for public hearings before permits could be issued. Even so, Illinois farmers and environmentalists asked for even stricter laws. Their demands were met in 1975 with amendments requiring mine operators to remove topsoil and replace it after mining in an effort to restore mine land to row-crop production.

Those were steps forward from the early days, when many sites were left in very raw condition. According to Jennifer Kulier's article "From Wastelands to Wetlands," one observer described an abandoned surface-mine site saying it was, "Like Hell with the fires put out." During those early days of mining, the goal was to work fast, get the coal, and move on. Mine operators left behind huge piles of shale and rock. Topsoil was buried. Clay was everywhere. Banks around these early mine sites were often bare, with acidic soils and water that sometimes ran red, orange, and purple. Even sites that had vegetation growing, eventually, were hard to use. Hills and steep-sided lakes made access difficult and growing crops impossible. This was land use in the extreme — and not in complimentary terms. The same thing was happening across the country, though things were better in Illinois by the 1970s, thanks to the early and groundbreaking state legislation.

Even so, by the late 1970s, more than 200,000 acres had been impacted by surface mines or deep coal mines in Illinois and the IDNR said 22,000 acres were identified as "problem" acreage. That meant the property had exposed refuse, tipple sites or sparsely vegetated spoil banks and had adversely affected water and land. So federal reclamation legislation made a difference in Illinois, too.

You can see the impact of different mining laws across the state. Actually, if you have knowledge of the years when different laws were passed, you can even tell when properties were mined. Do you see lots of jagged, saw-tooth ridges? That's old surface-mine ground. Does the land have narrow expanses of flat ground atop a ridge? That's 1960s surface-mine ground. Hard to tell it was mined? That's post-law ground, mined after 1977. And that's how Quail Lakes looks today.

While Illinois was moving forward with reclamation laws, the same was not true across the U.S. Because laws varied so widely from state to state, mining companies could move locations to take advantage of less strict laws. Colorado had voluntary reclamation laws that mine companies could heed or not as they saw fit. Since reclamation added cost to an already low-margin venture, most opted not to volunteer. That wide variance in state laws was a rallying point for environmentalists seeking federal oversight. So began a classic fight between the federal government and states' rights.

The battle through Washington was not easy, either, and raged from 1968 to 1977. The environmental movement was still gaining strength in the 1970s, but was faced with serious policy issues that made going green less popular. I remember the long gas lines and expensive gas prices when I first moved to Peoria in the mid-1970s. There was a government-induced shortage of fuel even though the entire world knew there was a surplus of oil and gasoline at the time. It was a mess. Since that first energy shock of the 1970s we've had an ongoing debate about using energy versus balancing environmental concerns.

The other side is that our economy has been so strong here in the United States in part because we've had cheap and abundant energy and coal has always been a huge source of that energy. That's one thing that has made this country what it is. So we've got to be careful with that balance. The tradeoff between conservation and clean energy is at the heart of the debate. But as in most things, it's a balance that our society must achieve. And whether we are talking about an individual or a society, in my view the more affluent the person or society the greater the responsibility to pursue conservation.

But back in the 1970s, those economic woes and the energy crisis, real or artificial, stalled several attempts at federal surface-mining laws. President Gerald Ford vetoed federal bills proposing such regulation in 1974 and 1975. In explaining his second veto he wrote to Congress on May 20, 1975: "We can develop our energy sources while protecting our environment. But this bill does not do that. I have supported responsible action to control surface mining and to reclaim damaged land. I continue to support actions that strike a proper balance between our energy and economic goals and important environmental objectives. Unfortunately H.R. 25 does not strike such a balance. As the one abundant energy source over which the United States has total control, coal is critical to the achievement of American energy independence. In the face of our deteriorating energy situation, we must not arbitrarily place restrictions on the development of this energy resource."

It is interesting to read words from nearly 40 years ago that still resonate. Even so, in 1976, Jimmy Carter hit the campaign trail promising to sign surface-mine reclamation legislation. After being elected, President Carter made good on that promise on Aug. 3, 1977. He said, "Many years ago, because of my help and the help of many others, Georgia passed a very strong strip-mining law. And I know that many here have worked for six years, sometimes much longer, to get a federal strip-mining law which would be fair and reasonable, which would enhance the legitimate and much needed production of coal and, also, assuage the fears that the beautiful areas where coal is produced were being destroyed. This has been in many ways a disappointing effort. The Congress has passed legislation that would meet these needs. Unfortunately, in the past, the bills have been vetoed. But I found, as I campaigned around our nation for two years, that there's an overwhelming, favorable sentiment among the people of our country that this legislation be passed."

With the law signed, mine operators had to learn a new set of rules. SMCRA changed surface mining forever by creating the Office of Surface Mining and establishing federal standards for reclamation. The Act also created a program to reclaim abandoned mine lands. Interestingly, many federal rules and regulations were drawn directly from the Illinois SMLCRA of 1975. This was good legislation that has greatly lessened the impact of surface mining.

Doug Oberhelman

Quail Lakes is a great example of what the federal reclamation act (SMCRA) meant for mine operators, as our property was among the first in central Illinois to be mined with the 1977 law in place. The legislation required various dramatic changes in how the miners approached a property. Runoff water had to be impounded. Nearby residents had to be given daily notice about blasting. Under SMCRA, prospective mine operators had plenty of work to do before they ever obtained a mining permit. They were required to restore the land to a condition capable of supporting the use it supported prior to mining or to "higher or better uses."

How was that defined? Among the requirements was a comprehensive plan for reclaiming the land, based on a survey and an inventory of the pre-mining condition and wildlife present. That's according to Christy, who had a unique perspective on reclamation. An Indiana native who graduated from Purdue University with a background in agronomy, Christy worked for the state of Illinois from 1966 to 1977 enforcing mine reclamation laws. After passage of the SMCRA, he was offered a job working for ASARCO and Midland Coal Company as a farm and reclamation director. "I took off my white hat and put on my black hat," he joked.

Having an understanding of both production and enforcement helped Christy. "When you're looking at getting a permit, you're basically looking at your cropland before and you pretty much need to put that back acre for acre," he observed. "Then you look at the pasture, timber and whatever else there is. You are normally trying to put most all of your pasture back. What you're going to end up with afterwards is water that's probably going to come out of your timber ground. So if you've got 60 acres of cropland, 20 acres of pasture and 20 acres of timber before [mining], you're going to come back with 60 acres of cropland, 20 acres of pasture, 10 acres of water and 10 acres of timber." Cropland was sacred.

Only after completing the plan could operators post what was called a performance bond — insurance that would allow the government to pay for reclamation should a mining company fail. After a mining company met all reclamation requirements, bonds were released and money was returned. That cash was a powerful incentive. Phase I considerations for reclamation included backfilling, regrading, topsoil replacement, and

Cattails wave in the breeze on the shores of Cabin Lake, in whose deep, clear waters rainbow trout are able to live year-round despite the heat of an Illinois summer. Photo courtesy of Ben Bean/Caterpillar Inc.

drainage control. Land had to be restored to the approximate original contour. Drainage and erosion had to be minimized. By satisfying Phase I, up to 60 percent of a bond could be released. Phase II required that vegetation had to be established, erosion had to be limited, and prime farmland had to reach certain yield levels. At this point, 25 percent more of the bond money could be released. Then in Phase III the established vegetation was required to meet certain yields per acre (for corn and soybeans) to release remaining bond funds.

At Quail Lakes, the first step was to build a sedimentation pond on the east side of the property to collect runoff. "We always put those sediment ponds in lower places," Miars explained. The stipulation for mines was that any water running off the site had to first pass through a pond.

"There was no water in the mine that ran off the mine that didn't go through a pond," Grimm said. "I look at all these farm fields and in the spring with these heavy rains, there's erosion all over." Not at the mine.

The next step was to start stockpiling topsoil for reclamation. But Midland Coal had actually started setting aside topsoil in 1975, two years prior to the 1977 ruling. "The state implemented a law that went into effect in July of 1976 that required topsoil removal and replacement. And ASARCO, or Midland, had no resistance to it," Christy recalled. "They started picking up topsoil in the fall of 1975 even before they had to. I was always shocked at that." Thank goodness they did, though. Having that topsoil to put back on top of the ground after mining has made a huge difference in our ability to restore Quail Lakes. It's really what got us started since the heavy dirt work was already done.

Prior to mining, the state checked topsoil depths. According to Miars, depths at Quail Lakes ranged from 4-10 inches. "We stockpiled the topsoil in a place where we were not going to strip the ground. At [Quail Lakes] that meant the soil was piled within 100 feet of the road, since that could not be stripped," Miars recalled. "We ran Cat 631 scrapers and after we stockpiled the dirt there were huge piles. I mean huge piles of dirt." There was so much topsoil, in fact, that operators had some left over when reclamation was complete. That explains why the far western reaches of Quail Lakes along Illinois Route 78 are higher than other parts of the property.

"That's one thing we're blessed with in Illinois is good materials. We've got probably 15 inches of topsoil here and then you have your windblown materials from the glacial viewpoint," Christy said. "This property here, we had a lot of good materials to start with so we didn't have a lot of problems with that."

At Quail Lakes the crews ran four bulldozers and four scrapers throughout first and second shifts. Service was done on third shift. "All the dozers we used were white. They made that some kind of reclamation law, you couldn't use a white dozer in the pit," Miars remembered. I still know of many white Caterpillar dozers around the world and we still offer white paint as an option. Mines like them mainly because the white offers a stark contrast to the black coal.

Only after the topsoil was stockpiled and set aside could the next phase of mining start: removal of the overburden — rock and other materials covering the coal. At Quail Lakes, the shovel, the wheel, and the dragline removed overburden. Then the coal came out. During reclamation, overburden was returned to the pit from which the coal was removed. Then subsoil and topsoil were placed on top of the rocky overburden. "After you stripped the ground you came in with dozers

Quail Lakes & Coal

Diane and I pose with our old Labrador retriever Sadie in the goose pit we call 'Chesapeake,' which is on Big Lake.

and leveled off the ground as best you could," Miars said. "And you have to have at least 30 inches of clay material above the rock. After you got it leveled the state came in with a backhoe and checked to make sure there was 30 inches of clay before you could put the topsoil back. And they would check random spots. If you found one rock in those 30

Doug Oberhelman

A Caterpillar D9 pulls a deep ripper through a wheat stubble field at Quail Lakes. The ripper helped loosen soil that had been compacted by scrapers and other machinery during reclamation. Photo courtesy of Phil Christy.

inches you had to tear out an area and then get it back to level. The state and the EPA required that. It was a pain, it really was. If they found one rock you had to redo an area. It seemed to me like it was a 10-by-10 piece."

After the inspectors were done, soil could be put back in place. For areas that had four inches of topsoil prior to mining, operators added four inches of topsoil. One factor working in favor of early mine efforts at Quail Lakes was that Bill Threw, a former landowner on the far north end, had requested a large T-shaped lake be built. That meant instead of filling the pit once the coal was gone, workers could simply leave it open and keep mining south. That saved time and helps explain some of the leftover topsoil.

Today the former Threw parcel is part of Quail Lakes and we call it Northwest Lake. We put an aerator on the lake in the winter to keep the water from freezing and you can't believe how many geese and ducks will pack into that water. We have seen many times in January when everything else was completely frozen and there was not another square inch of open water available for another giant Canada goose. And to think, if Bill Threw had not requested the lake, the mine would have filled it with shale, clay, and topsoil and it would just have been another tillable field. What a great idea!

There are six other sizable ponds or lakes on the property, one of which was the old sediment lake Miars mentioned. We call that Crappie Lake, because it provides some great crappie fishing. We've worked hard to improve water quality in that lake by building dry dams and terraces upstream in the watershed to slow the flow of water and silt into the lake. Not far from Crappie Lake is our Wood Duck Hole, which we created by building a dam at the end of a tree-filled ravine. Thanks to the efforts of a beaver, we don't have near as many trees in that lake any longer. But we do still see plenty of wood ducks. We also have Frog Pond near Northwest Lake, which is a shallower body of water that's lined with cattails and attracts frogs and other amphibians. I remember to this day a wonderful evening of frog gigging with Diane and our good friend Jim Hardesty. We still laugh out loud over that outing. There's also a smaller lake in the southwest corner of the property that has been overrun with muskrats in recent years. Sometimes creating habitat can be a headache, but any time I see wildlife I smile.

The last two lakes — Cabin Lake and Big Lake — are final-cut lakes that are 65 feet deep. Final-cut lakes typically are built in the last area that is mined on a site, which at Quail Lakes was in the south and east of the property. Final cuts are almost never filled back in because of the expense, according to Grimm. "When you start that first cut you've got to throw it somewhere. So every time you cut, you are throwing that dirt somewhere behind you. With that last cut, we always went for a lake, because otherwise where are you going to get the dirt to fill that lake?" Grimm asked. "You just never have dirt to fill a final cut. So people hardly ever fill final cuts. It's too expensive. When you get a permit for this, if there's 300 acres of cropland, that's not negotiable. Let's say that leaves you 200 acres of wooded acres or draws or pastures. Those are the areas where you have some flexibility in permitting. That's where you can say we are going to take some of this wooded area and make it into a final-cut lake."

We have a cabin on the north shore of Cabin Lake. Big Lake is in the southeast corner of the property. Like most final-cut lakes, both are deep, clear and cold and hold plenty of water. Grimm explained there was initially concern about whether Cabin Lake would fill in a timely fashion. But it did and is the one lake that never seems to change in its water level. There must be a powerful spring in there somewhere. Today Cabin Lake is home to rainbow trout, which is significant since they need cold water to survive the long hot summers typical of Illinois. These lakes are also among the last to freeze in the area, which means ducks and geese linger there longer than at many other places. It's worth noting that final-cut lakes differ in one other significant way. Lakes that are mined with a shovel have at one end a shallow, gradual rise out of the water. That rise was necessary so the shovel could walk itself out of the pit. No gradual rise is needed for lakes mined by the dragline because a dragline does not sit on the coal. So these are typically very steep-sided bodies of water.

That was the case in Big Lake, where we have a goose pit that is also featured on the cover of this book. We call that "Chesapeake" because of a story told to Diane, Jerry Foley and me by our friend who built the pit. He said the pit was designed "just like the ones in the Chesapeake Bay." Well, we never believed much that he told us, but he really told good stories. Midland Coal planted trees around the lake as part of reclamation. We have added native prairie plantings around the perimeter of those trees, creating a haven for bobwhite quail, deer, and other wildlife.

Aside from the lakes, most of the terrain at Quail Lakes looks very much like it did in the 1950s and 60s when it was being farmed. The topography had to be within 15 percent of original. If there were slopes and rolling hills prior to mining, there had to be slopes and rolling hills after mining. The major difference was that everything was elevated a bit, owing to the swell factor present in mining. Grimm said the acceptable swell factor was about 20 percent and occurs because rock, clay and soil placed back in a pit has not had time to settle and compact. So it stands taller than before mining. But in essence, the reflection of the topography was the same, just at a higher elevation.

Once inspectors had signed off on land, it could be planted to row crops. "The first crop was wheat," Christy recalled. "You would spread topsoil through the summer and then be ready to plant wheat and leave it on through the winter. That helped with erosion control and you could also get a decent crop out of it." The mines would also plant alfalfa hay to stabilize the soil. After two or three years a deep tillage unit was brought in and pulled by a D9 dozer. Only then did they consider planting corn and beans, which are harder to grow on reclaimed mine ground.

Before surety bonds were released, tillable land classified as high-capability cropland had to produce 90 percent of the county average for three different crops. Acres that were classified as prime farmland had to come back to 100 percent of the county average for one year in 10. "It's going to take you generally five to six years to get through that scenario to get 90 percent yield," Christy said.

Waterways and non-crop areas were planted in alfalfa, brome, and orchard grass seeded by airplane in mid-March to take advantage of spring freeze-and-thaw cycles. Terraces were built to slow the runoff of water from agricultural fields. Dry dams were also used to slow the flow.

At Quail Lakes the mine created a series of dry dams that we now call our Lower Wetlands. "We put those dry dams in on the presumption they would silt in and kind of eliminate the dam," Christy noted. "Well, Grimm did such a good job we had very little erosion and very good growth of vegetation." We have since reworked those dry dams using designs drawn up by the Peoria County office of the Natural Resources Conservation Service. But the mine's original contours allowed us to install agri-drains to control the water.

We also planted the area with native prairie plants, and there's one stretch where huge Maximilian sunflowers dominate the landscape in August. They are really spectacular and provide food for all kinds of birds. And there is still water that collects behind those dry dams in wet years, providing habitat for many waterfowl species and shorebirds. We frequently see teal and gadwall broods in the spring and this is also a favorite stopover for snow geese. Diane, Allen and I — along with our black Labrador retrievers Dozer and Diesel, and before them Sadie — have had some great early teal season shoots around the cattails there.

Getting native grasses and forbs to grow is one thing, but raising crops is another — even with the topsoil returned. "If someone wanted to argue it was not as good of cropland as before, they could," Grimm agreed. "When you get a drought year, that subsoil just doesn't have the structure to hold water." No wonder. It took thousands of years to create the rich, black soils that produce bumper crops of corn and beans. It's hard to expect ground that was mined to be as fertile in the first few years after the dragline leaves.

Doug Oberhelman

That's one of the main reasons we are so pleased with a relationship we have with our neighbors, Elmwood Farms LLC, a 1,200-cow dairy that produces on average 85,000 pounds of milk per day. Of that, 85 percent is sold in Peoria under the Prairie Farms label and 15 percent is sold in St. Louis as Dean's milk. Having a dairy nearby works very well for us and for them. The crops we raise are used to feed the dairy herd. The waste they produce is used to improve our soil. It's a great symbiotic setup. Eventually, Quail Lakes would be back to the same productive, fertile black soil it was before mining. We gave it a jump-start with the dairy cycle.

Sam Dilsaver has run the dairy since 2007 when he came to Illinois from California. He started when he was just 23, and he has done a great job. Sam appreciates our relationship too. We get along great and it is helping bring to life another chapter in the evolving story of Quail Lakes. "The nice thing with strip-mine ground is that it needs a lot of fertility. And it takes like 50 years to overload the soil," Dilsaver marveled. " We have to watch the nitrogen level [when we apply manure] and we can't put on more nitrogen than we are going to take off. But as far as the [phosphorous] and [potassium], obviously we have to obey the guidelines. But I've been told by our soil guy that you could really put an endless amount on the soil for 20 years without hurting the soil."

Diane hoists a nice northern pike she caught in the fall at our Middle Grove lake, which was mined in the 1920s and was not reclaimed.

Manure is pumped from a large lagoon at the dairy onto crop fields each fall after the corn comes out. All the waste is applied precisely and controlled so there's no runoff. The Environmental Protection Agency monitors things closely and stipulates a nutrient management plan the

Quail Lakes & Coal

dairy must follow. Typically we have about 600 acres planted in corn that is cut for silage to feed the dairy herd. That can happen as early as July or as late as the end of August. When the weather cooperates, Sam likes to plant wheat after the soil has dried from the fall application of manure. Then in the spring he can apply more manure to the wheat. "That's one of the main reasons we want to plant wheat. Because we can get rid of more manure," Dilsaver noted. "Not that we can't spring-apply to corn ground, but our corn is already off and we like to get all that done in the fall to let it freeze and thaw."

There are risks to planting wheat. "If you have a wet spring and then go pump 15,000 to 20,000 gallons per acre and that's got to dry and then you get rain it just makes it that much worse," Dilsaver cautioned. "If you can't get in to harvest the wheat it puts everything back. And then you're planting corn in July."

Another 100 acres of Quail Lakes cropland is planted in alfalfa hay, a crop that thrives on old surface mine ground. In a year with decent moisture, Dilsaver expects to get seven cuttings: "Hay just loves strip mine ground. It thrives on it. We'll cut it every 28 days and [in 2012] we started in April and we'll go until September or October depending on the weather."

One other interesting side note about the dairy is that they've got two Caterpillar generators. Manure from the cows creates methane gas, which is burned by the generators and creates electricity — up to 1 kilowatt for every 13 cows. We're proud of this. Milk is a staple of everyday life and by using the methane byproduct the dairy is again conserving our atmosphere.

While large-scale dairies are not real popular, they are only filling the demand for milk. If someone wants to pay $6 a gallon for milk that is certified organic, there's a place for that. Most people don't want to pay that or can't afford to pay that. Those people appreciate access to relatively inexpensive milk produced by large-scale farmers who are highly regulated and — for the most part — have a pretty good environmental track record. These dairies are filling the demand for milk at a very low cost.

And I think they do a good job of controlling their environment. The EPA pays close attention to large dairies. In the case of Elmwood Farms, everything I have seen gives me reason to believe there's no cause for worry. I've watched our neighbor be very cautious, responsive, and committed to ensuring his footprint is minimal. And it works so darn well. It helps the ground and the crops we raise sustain that dairy. So it's a symbiotic process when all is said and done — but a process that does require committed owners and diligent managers to make it work well.

There's no question all that manure from the dairy has made our cropland more productive. Even without the dairy, the ground at Quail Lakes is in stark contrast to other nearby sites mined prior to 1977. In fact, just a few hundred feet west of Quail Lakes across Illinois Route 78 you can see thousands of acres that were mined in the 1960s. On these older mine sites there's very little tillable ground and the evidence of stripping is clear in high-sided, saw-toothed banks, exposed shale and limited contouring of the land. Midland Coal also mined these properties, but they did so under different reclamation laws. Instead of saving all of the topsoil, they merely made a pass or two along ridges to flatten them out. While these old mines have great populations of wildlife, they really can't sustain tillable acreage.

This obvious contrast in reclamation styles was an educational tool for Grimm, who, "always enjoyed taking people down this road when we would give company-wide tours. I always went down [Route 78] after we were done and it was in farm ground. And I would say, 'Look at what strip mining did west of 78.'" Then Grimm would point to the Quail Lakes property on the east side of Illinois 78 where corn and beans grew bountifully. He would ask, "What do you think of this?" Recalled Grimm, "They would say, 'That looks like good farm ground.' And I'd say, "That was stripped too.' It was just a beautiful comparison!"

I couldn't agree more. Diane and I also own surface-mine property near Middle Grove that was mined in the 1920s. That was long before reclamation laws and the difference between the properties is night and day. That Middle Grove property has deep, steep banks and much of the property is hard to hike through. There's no question that the 1977 reclamation laws make a dramatic difference. But that rougher Middle Grove property also proves what nature can do when given the chance. We've got very good deer and turkey populations at Middle Grove. And the mile-long lake has a healthy population of northern pike, muskie, bass, and big crappie. We appreciate the fishing there, too, particularly

Diane who has a real knack for catching northern pike in the fall. We've even seen bald eagles sitting on the ice in the winter. All that is thanks to Mother Nature.

The same story on a larger scale played out at Kickapoo State Park near Danville in east-central Illinois, which is home to some of the country's original surface mines. Between 1860 and 1940, much of Kickapoo State Park was surface-mined for coal. There were no reclamation laws in those days and spoil piles and mine pits were left behind with little thought for the environment. But to visit the 2,842-acre park today is to visit a recreational mecca. Twisting through the spoils are trails for running and hiking and sites for camping and hunting. The lakes offer canoeing, scuba diving, and fishing for trout and other species. There are 22 lakes on the property and trees are everywhere. Overall the rugged topography of the site has gone from a scary moonscape to an appealing tree-covered wilderness that attracts recreational users and wildlife in great numbers. According to IDNR, Kickapoo State Park is also historic in that it is believed to be the nation's first park built on ground that was surface mined. And it was one of the first to be subsidized through public contributions as Danville residents made contributions to finance the original purchase of 1,290 acres from United Electric Coal Co. in 1939.

Diane didn't hesitate to jump in and drive this Cat 420 backhoe. We use this machine frequently while working to improve erosion control at Quail Lakes.

There are similar stories of surface-mined properties being used for parks all across Illinois. In fact, many of the finest recreation areas in the state were mined. Some were reclaimed; some were old mines that simply needed time to heal. Healing also happened on private ground, on those ugly, scarred properties of the 1940s, 50s and 60s. "When you were done you had this ugly looking pile after pile after pile. It looked like a moonscape almost," noted Richard Coon, who worked on Knox County mines for parts of years before becoming a wildlife biologist for the U.S. Fish and Wildlife Service. "But the mine had no obligation to put it back the way it was in those days. Nobody had held their feet to the fire yet. Well, people thought given enough time, land is forgiving. Over time something good will happen for that land. What do we see now? We see these hunting and fishing clubs. We see cattle ranches. You see waterfowl. You see a great blue heron flying over the road in a place you wouldn't have seen a great blue heron flying over otherwise. It's diversity."

Reclaimed mines have been used for more than wildlife habitat. In the Chicago area, surface mines have also been converted to housing developments and schools, golf courses, shopping centers, industrial developments, athletic fields, and more according to the Illinois State Geological Survey's publication *Geology of Illinois*. Some reclamation projects have even won awards, such as those received by the Max McGraw Wildlife Foundation for its work on former sand and gravel pits near Elgin, Illinois. Diane and I are members of the Max McGraw Wildlife Foundation — a wonderful organization that provides much-needed conservation education to so many.

In our case at Quail Lakes, we got a considerable head start thanks to reclamation laws. I started acquiring the property to create Quail Lakes in 1996 before I married Diane. We completed our acquisitions in 2010. We could have been content to merely fish and hunt and make money off the tillable ground. But we saw opportunity to improve the land even after the old mine site was released from bonds. We started prairie plantings in 2003-04 with help from the folks at Pheasants Forever and our local office of the NRCS. Pheasants Forever supplied the knowledge and the planting drill and we supplied the seed. The folks at Pheasants Forever really do know a lot about native plants and how to get them to grow. I also owe brothers Ted and Ron Gilles much credit for showing us the way to get started.

In the past few years Bill Atwood and I have planted numerous grass waterways at Quail Lakes. We planted a 10-foot grass buffer around agricultural fields to slow soil erosion. Coincidentally, those plantings also offer great paths for the four-wheelers we ride while checking out Quail Lakes! We've added wetlands in areas that did not drain well and have installed five agri-drains to help control water. One of those was an old bubbling spring. It was useless ground so we put a dam on both sides and an agri-drain in there and it works great. "This is a whole different type of soil. Normally you can go out and run a tile and drain a spot. But this ground won't leech through the tile right," Atwood explained. "So instead we let it run off and collect it. Otherwise it just puddles."

My aim is zero erosion on our property. And we're getting there. We're on the last end of our erosion control and it is really rewarding to think that place was open 75 feet down and now we're just about to the point where you don't get any erosion. Plus, erosion control can even be scenic. When Diane and I spend time at Quail Lakes we make a point to go out on our four-wheelers to see all the wildflowers and prairie grasses we've planted.

Atwood, Diane and I have also continued to plant native prairie plants throughout the property. "We did a lot of that with a seeder on a four-wheeler," Atwood recalled. "Some years I think the plants came up better using the four-wheeler than with the drill." One favorite plant I see regularly is the big Maximilian sunflower. They're huge and really stand out. I also like the purple coneflower and the gray-headed coneflower, which has a nice yellow flower. You can see a lot of those in our Lower Wetlands. That's also a good place to see big bluestem, the grass that Avery Dalton and his family helped plow under more than 170 years ago. In some places, we didn't even have to plant a thing. Somehow the seeds were just there in the soil.

This has really been rewarding work because in no time the areas we have disturbed have typically grown up in sunflowers, cattails, and other plants. It's amazing how fast the earth can heal itself. When I retire, I've got plans for plenty more projects; enough that Bill gets a bit worried. "You keep telling me we're going to have fun when you retire. I say, 'We? Do you have a bird in your pocket?'" Atwood joked.

For us, the continued restoration has become almost an obsession. Perhaps obsession is a bit too strong, but we want to have a showpiece property with a working farm and a non-working farm that offers wildlife habitat and trophy conservation efforts. One thing has led to another out there. The real catalyst for our work was when we built the first part of the Lower Wetlands. It's in the southwest corner of the property and had been an area that did not drain well. It wasn't really serving any role on the farm, so we decided to make it a wetland. This was a spot that had been mined and had been farmed and plowed over and disked. Through all that, all we did was dam it up and put a little water on it. We finished that in mid-summer a few years ago. And then, wham, up came the cattails. I couldn't believe it. It wasn't 30 days and cattails were coming up all over. How does that happen? Where did those seeds and roots come from anyway?

Well, the next spring the place was covered with ducks migrating through. We'd never really seen many ducks in that part of the farm. Then all of the sudden it was holding teal, mallards, widgeon — you name it, we saw them. It was really awesome. And all we had to do was build a small dam and put some water on it to create excellent waterfowl habitat. That was something that was a real catalyst for me and for Diane.

In the summer of 2012, I was invited to speak at the annual Ducks Unlimited convention. One of the things I said was that people with the interest and the means have a higher obligation to conservation than anyone else. I really believe that. Someone has to step up. The nice thing is that the reclamation work the mine did and the prairie plantings and wetland creation we've done have set up a buffet table for wildlife, perhaps even greater than when Avery Dalton arrived more than 170 years ago.

CHAPTER FIVE

THE WILDLIFE RESPONDS

In the past few years, several proposed surface mines in Illinois met with heated opposition from people calling themselves environmentalists. Opponents have cited what they see as numerous "environmental concerns" stemming from surface mining. In the case of a proposed mine near Banner, Illinois, opponents stressed the impact mining might have on nesting by bald eagles and ospreys. One who spoke against the proposed mine told the *Peoria Journal Star* that the area is home to migratory waterfowl and other wildlife and "should be preserved for wildlife and not stripped." Another person noted that it could damage habitat for ground-nesting short-eared owls.

In southern Illinois, a proposed land swap between the U.S. Forest Service and Peabody Energy generated widespread negative reaction in 2012. Word that Peabody hopes to mine 384 acres on both sides of the Saline River in Gallatin County was not received well. "A strip mine changes the topography of the land forever. It is probably the most devastating thing that can occur on the land," argued Sam Stearns in an article in the *Harrisburg Daily Register*.

Really? Comments like those make me wonder whether the people claiming these things have ever visited a surface mine after the dragline, scrapers, and dozers finished their work. Not immediately, of course. At first, there's no question the land looks different. You can't dig down 75-100 feet into the ground, pile things up and then smooth things over again without altering the landscape.

But given time, the restored grass grows. Trees grow. And in those grassy acres surrounding surface mines and final-cut lakes you'll find more wildlife and in greater variety than just about anywhere else in Illinois. For wild animals, surface mines provide a habitat oasis on an Illinois landscape that (outside of cities, towns, and urban areas) otherwise consists mainly of corn and beans. Do you want to know why there's even a discussion of short-eared owls near that proposed mine near Banner? It's because of the grasslands that grew after nearby land was surface mined for coal. Do you know where some of those eagles and ospreys are nesting? They nest above lakes that were created during the process of surface mining for coal.

This is no isolated instance. Scientific reports abound lauding the wildlife benefits of surface mines. Mined properties — both reclaimed and those that are not reclaimed — provide benefits for virtually all types of wild creatures native to Illinois, whether birds, reptiles, amphibians, insects or mammals. I've seen it with my own eyes.

Veteran mine reclamation inspector and manager Phil Christy summarized things well when he disputed claims that surface mines are bad for wildlife. "I don't understand why the wildlife societies, the Audubon Society, and the others, fight surface mining. That makes no sense at all," Christy asserted. "Millions of acres of wildlife habitat have been created by mining. What you end up with is a very diverse environment where before in many cases it was a mono-culture, at least where you are dealing with farmland."

Diane holds a duck retrieved by our old Labrador retriever Sadie at Quail Lakes.

Or as long-time mine manager and worker Jim Grimm noted, "People give me a hard time, kiddingly, about ruining cropland. I say, 'Well, we created animal habitat.'"

That's no joke. I always smile when I think about the coal being gone from under Quail Lakes. Otherwise I would not even know that property today.

At Quail Lakes we get the best of all worlds. Energy. Crops. Fishing. And wildlife. In the end, Grimm had it exactly right. He did build

Quail Lakes & Coal

Allen Cullinan retrieves a blue-winged teal in his bare feet during one of many memorable hunts at Quail Lakes.

Allen and I are all smiles after bagging a blue-wing in our Lower Wetlands, which offers great shallow-water habitat for teal and other migrating shorebirds.

wildlife habitat. Just look at what we have today on our 1,200 acres. When's the last time you saw an eagle or an osprey around a cornfield? Never? Yet you will see those same birds at former surface mines all over Illinois. At many sites they are even building nests and raising young. That includes Banner Marsh State Fish and Wildlife Area, former surface-mine ground just 14 miles south of ours.

Diane made a fantastic 75-yard shot on this snow goose at our Lower Wetlands. In recent years we've seen more snow geese at Quail Lakes.

We also see eagles on a regular basis around Quail Lakes. Those birds rely heavily on fish in their diet. They find fish in surface-mine lakes. We've even seen osprey at Quail Lakes during their fall migration. I'll never forget that. We stood right outside our cabin and an osprey sat on a post in our dove field. He just sat there for the longest time. We absolutely could not believe we had an osprey on our own land, miles from any "big water."

And there are more endangered species than eagles or osprey that benefit from surface mines. Ever see an endangered short-eared owl? You can in the grass fields around Banner Marsh, at the Metropolitan Sanitary District's complex near Cuba, and at grasslands across Peoria, Knox, and Fulton counties. Guess what those properties share in common. They were surface mines. After the miners left, grass was allowed to grow and the owls found that habitat oasis in a landscape otherwise devoted to row crops. Don't get me wrong — I am not against farming. Far from it. Having grown up the son of an agricultural equipment salesman, I know firsthand how critical it is for us to have enough cropland to sustain the nation.

But short-eared owls need large blocks of undisturbed grasslands, not narrow ditches or patches here and there. They find what they need in former surface mines. That's why it seems ironic that so-called environmentalists would fight a surface mine on behalf of a bird that in Illinois relies on them for a place to live! The same storyline is true for harrier hawks, another state-threatened species. They are regulars around Quail Lakes, cruising over the grassy areas searching for mice and snakes. They are so majestic and so different from the red-tailed hawks we see all the time.

Beyond state-endangered birds are several you just don't commonly see in central Illinois. Quail Lakes attracts them, too. We've seen loons and trumpeter swans. Would they have been there if the area had never been surface mined? I doubt it. No wonder birdwatchers in the Peoria area make regular outings to surface mines to see birds they can't find anywhere else in the Illinois landscape. What else? We regularly encounter young broods of blue-winged teal and gadwall. The green heron is Diane's favorite bird and we see those almost every day. Another favorite at Quail Lakes are kingbirds. They are all over and they are the neatest little guys. They have a nice call and are friendly. But I don't see them many other places — only out here at what others originally viewed as a "devastated" surface mine.

Yes, surface mining disturbs wildlife in the short term. Blasting often moves animals away from mine sites. Blasting is also an issue with nearby human residents. But in terms of wildlife, our experience at Quail Lakes suggests the long-term gains far outweigh the short-term issues. Drive through central Illinois sometime. Pay attention to where you see birds and beasts. In cornfields? Bean fields? Not so much. When you enter surface-mine country you start to see wild creatures. Waterfowl. Wild turkey. Deer. And many others. That's as true in central Illinois as it is in southern Illinois, or southeastern Illinois.

For me, one of the best times to be in surface-mine country is in the fall, while ducks and geese of all sorts are passing through. Spend a September day there and you might be buzzed by flocks of migrating teal. First come the blue-winged teal headed south. They stay only briefly in Illinois but make the most of exposed mudflats. We've had wonderful teal hunts early in the year with just a handful of decoys

Doug Oberhelman

tossed out in the Lower Wetlands. Diane's son Allen even did the retrieving there one year in his bare feet. We still laugh about that.

After blue-wings come the early migrants in October: gadwall, shovelers, green-winged teal, pintails, and widgeon. By November, mallards start to arrive, though they are coming later and later every year. Then as the ice forms diver ducks make an appearance, attracted to the deep water of final-cut lakes that freeze later than other lakes and rivers in the area. Canvasbacks are annual visitors to Big Lake and we've got three from a hunt mounted in our cabin. Redheads also like the deep water, including one Diane shot at sunset that our older Labrador retriever Sadie retrieved from 500 yards away.

For Diane and me, the steady stream of migrants is very gratifying. As longtime supporters of Ducks Unlimited and as a member of Wetlands Trust America, we are passionate about helping waterfowl. The surface-mine properties we own provide critical migration habitat in both the fall and spring. Additional wetlands we've created at Quail Lakes only add to the diversity of duck species we see. In recent years we've also been treated to visits by huge flocks of white-fronted geese and snow geese.

There are year-round waterfowl residents too, in particular the resident giant Canada geese that are such a welcome sight for hunters and birdwatchers alike. We sure enjoy them and Diane is always leading the charge on our hunts, whether in our pit, our blind or our layout blinds. And the early season hunting is a sight to behold. We've shot five-bird limits multiple times in the silage fields when the geese are still young and naive. They don't stay that way forever, though. Every year since 1996 we have put out nesting structures for Canada geese and changed the straw in them. We've got around 12 nests. If you multiply 12 broods every year by five goslings each, you can start to see just how many geese we've helped hatch. Many other surface-mine owners have done the same thing for years and this has helped develop a huge flock of local "giants."

Even without landowner help, giant Canada geese were already among the biggest beneficiaries of surface mining. Before settlers started plowing and draining the wetlands of Illinois, these swampy areas were critical nesting areas for birds of all sorts, including giant Canada geese. In the late 1800s, Harold C. Hanson of the Illinois Natural History Survey said the Kankakee River Marshes in Indiana and Illinois were likely the most important breeding areas of the giant Canada goose in the Midwest. But as marshes were drained and agriculture spread, geese disappeared. With no wetlands, there was nowhere for the geese to nest safely. Populations dwindled. Hunters took a toll on the big birds by bagging as many as they wanted, with little or no attention to limits.

By the early 1900s the giant Canada goose in Illinois was believed to be virtually extinct. The same was thought to be true throughout the Midwest until Hanson studied a flock of geese that lived in a city park in Rochester, Minnesota. Eventually, researchers documented that these birds were Branta canadensis maxima, the same subspecies that had been native to much of the U.S. and to Illinois. By 1965, Hanson estimated that there were 55,000 wild giant Canada geese in Canada and the U.S., with 385 in Illinois.

As any resident or visitor to Illinois can tell you today, that's no longer the case. Giant Canada geese have made a remarkable comeback in the Prairie State and around the country. Today geese nest in all 102 Illinois counties and in every U.S. state and Canadian province. According to the IDNR, the Illinois resident goose population is estimated at well over 100,000 and local birds make up 40-50 percent of the annual harvest in the state. Given that, the comeback of the giant goose is often cited as a major victory of modern conservation. And in Illinois, surface-mine lakes played a critical role in that impressive comeback. That only makes sense. Look at the modern landscape. There are precious few marshes and wetlands. Historically, wetlands made up an estimated 23 percent of the surface area of Illinois. But from the 1780s to the 1980s as farming spread, we lost 85 percent of those wetlands — one of the greatest rates of loss in the U.S.

Surface-mined ground is not an ideal substitute for shallow wetlands, since the lakes are typically deep and are not well suited for emergent vegetation. But final-cut lakes offer what has turned out to be wonderful nesting habitat for geese — as well as for many other species of birds. The lakes provide water and islands and peninsulas offer grassy sanctuaries from predators. Well-grazed grassy areas around the lake offer perfect feeding areas for young goslings.

The first evidence of that came in the 1960s as Illinois began its giant goose restoration project in Fulton County. As you may recall from earlier chapters, Fulton, Knox, and Henry counties were dotted with numerous surface-mine lakes. In many ways, they mimic the pothole areas of the Dakotas, only without the abundant shallow-water wetland habitat. To establish populations, geese were confined at the surface mines, which biologists believed would be perfect goose habitat.

"A related benefit of the reintroduction effort was increased waterfowl use of thousands of acres of reclaimed surface-mined land," wrote Bob Williamson in *Giant Canada Goose Restoration and Management in Illinois*. Williamson continued: "Most of these reclaimed strip-mine lands contained small lakes and ponds with surrounding uplands seeded to grass. On many areas, cattle grazing maintained a short grass height creating ideal netting and brood-rearing habitat for Canada geese. Islands and peninsulas formed by spoil deposition provided an abundance of suitable nest sites."

The first releases of birds were in Fulton and Knox counties. A total of 80 juvenile geese were placed in holding pens at four locations. Birds came from stock purchased from private breeders in Illinois in the 1950s. The geese were held in pens until the spring of 1969, after which 64 were released. As a result, several townships in Fulton, Knox, and Henry counties were closed to Canada goose hunting. From 1969 to 1972 another 400 geese were released in these counties. Around the same time the Illinois Department of Conservation released Canada geese at other mine sites in northeastern and southern Illinois.

One release was on Fulton County land owned by Freeman United Coal Company, just a few miles from a farm owned by the Schenck family. Eric Schenck is the Illinois regional biologist for Ducks Unlimited and grew up on that farm in the midst of one of Illinois most intensely mined counties. Eric told me he remembers lights from the dragline shining in his bedroom. He said windows in the house would rattle at times when blasting crews were working. Like many families in Fulton County, his was split between mining and farming: mining on his mother's side, farming on his father's side. It probably never occurred to him that someday his farm background would help restore waterfowl habitat on former surface mines in his own county!

But that's exactly what happened. As coal was mined, fields of corn and beans became grasslands and lakes. Ducks were naturally attracted to the wetlands. As it turned out, surface-mine lakes were fantastic nesting areas for geese. Goose releases went very well. So did stockings in Chicago. Some might say too well, as dealing with "nuisance geese" is now a common problem in suburban Chicago and around golf courses all over the state. By the 1980s, the state was relocating geese from suburban Chicago to unoccupied surface-mine areas. Between 1980-91, Williamson said nearly 8,000 honkers were relocated in 46 of 102 Illinois counties. Hunting seasons finally opened in 1982, but only after overcoming intense opposition.

"The public opposition to the hunting season was almost phenomenal," recalled Norm Emerick, a retired wildlife biologist who worked for the IDNR for nearly 30 years. "We'd have public meetings and the people were worried we were going to slaughter the geese, even though all we were talking about was a 10-day quota, a limited season where you had to bring your goose to Lakeland Park [in Canton] or call it in." Eventually, officials ordered the season to start. Hunters did not slaughter the geese. Instead, geese became wiser, as anyone who has hunted them will surely agree. By 1991 the giant Canada goose reintroduction program was deemed a success and ended.

Work to develop surface-mined areas for wildlife has not ceased. In July of 2005, Schenck invited me to the dedication of a Fulton County projected developed by Ducks Unlimited at the Double T State Fish and Wildlife Area near Canton. Double T consists of 1,961 acres of former surface mine. The name of the site comes from two huge, final-cut lakes that from the air look like a Double T. IDNR purchased the land from The Nature Conservancy to use as a waterfowl management area and refuge. DU has worked with the IDNR to restore shallow wetlands on the property. My combined interest in The Nature Conservancy and DU made for a perfect confluence of events for the dedication of this wonderful wetland.

One irony of surface-mine reclamation is that post-law ground does not provide as much wildlife habitat as does land mined prior to 1977. That's according to Emerick, whose job it was for several years to oversee mine reclamation as it related to wildlife. "The middle mining period where they just knocked off the spoils and planted it to grass, that was good habitat," Emerick emphasized. "Places like Double T that were mined later, they really don't have the wildlife habitat on them as

Doug Oberhelman

much. Most of it went back to row crop." That's true also of our Quail Lakes property. To really make reclaimed properties work well for wildlife, you need to create wetlands, plant native prairie grass, and allow some weedy, unkempt areas for wild animals to live. We're working hard to do just that.

That was the goal of the project we honored at the Double T dedication that day. Mike Hitchcock had funded much of the project at Double T. Mike owns a large scrap-iron business outside of Canton, is an avid hunter, a Ducks Unlimited donor, a great Caterpillar customer, and a personal friend with whom I have hunted. Like Diane and me, Mike owns former surface-mine land that he has developed for waterfowl and other wildlife at his own expense. In addition to money that Mike donated to the Double T wetlands projects, DU also used Caterpillar equipment from the CAT Rental Store owned by Altorfer's in East Peoria. Through an arrangement with Caterpillar and Altorfer's, DU received $50,000 credit for renting bulldozers, backhoes, and excavators they needed to create wetlands. They used this credit to restore habitat at several other wildlife areas along the Illinois River.

The partnership was so innovative that the Wildlife Management Institute in Washington, D.C. recognized DU, Hitchcock Scrap Yard, Caterpillar, and the IDNR in 2004 with the "Touchstone" award. In some ways, this recognition came as no surprise to me because this is the creativity and commitment I see every day in Caterpillar's employees, its dealers, and customers. At the dedication I also met John Tomke, former DU president and chairman of the board. He came all the way from Indiana on a hot summer day to attend that dedication. But that's what I've learned to expect from DU. My respect and appreciation for that organization continues to grow from interactions like that and is one reason I was proud to accept a position on their board of directors for the Wetlands America Trust, the land-holding branch of DU.

The wetlands created at Double T have provided many wildlife benefits; attracting many more species of waterfowl than might otherwise have visited a deep, steep-sided final cut lake. Swans have also been seen at Double T and at many other surface-mine properties. That's significant, since trumpeters are making a slow but steady comeback. Once a common pre-settlement species estimated to number over 100,000 in North America, trumpeters were hunted to the brink of extinction by the

1930s. Hat makers coveted quills and plumes from the swans while Europeans powdered their noses with puffs made from swan skins.

Thanks to captive breeding programs and various reintroduction efforts across the country, swans are recovering. And surface-mined properties provide the big birds — which can weigh 20-30 pounds and stand four feet tall — a place to relax during their spring and fall migrations. A common migrant in central Illinois, trumpeters are even more frequently spotted at Burning Star No. 5 in southern Illinois. As many as 300 swans at a time have flocked to that former mine in the month of January. Another flock of 135 swans spends winters at a reclaimed surface mine in Edgar County near Paris in eastern Illinois. The combination of water and nearby winter wheat fields is very appealing to the birds, according to researchers Mike Eichholz and Dana Varner of Southern Illinois University.

Waterfowl are hardly the only avian species that benefit from surface mining. Actually, gains are greater for grassland and marsh species. The loss of wetlands and prairie in Illinois is staggering and has a direct impact on the creatures that rely on those types of habitat. The most recent estimation of Illinois endangered species published by the IDNR lists 25 birds. Of those, several are grassland species, several are marsh species, and several are terns. At Quail Lakes we regularly see most of the endangered grassland birds and marsh birds. Granted, we have worked hard to create several areas of shallow wetlands that are not present in all surface mines. But I've seen American bitterns and least bitterns lurking in the reeds and cattails of surface-mine lakes all over central Illinois.

Grassland gains are even greater. Today just 1 percent of Illinois prairie remains from the vast acres that covered more than 60 percent of the state pre-settlement. That has had a devastating impact on grassland species. But surface mines provide hope. Do an Internet search for "surface mine" and "grassland bird" and you will find numerous scientific studies showing the obvious benefits of undisturbed grassland. Fairly typical are the conclusions by Daniel W. Brauning, wildlife diversity division chief for the Pennsylvania Game Commission. His research showed that reclaimed mine land provides habitat for a diverse array of grassland bird species, species that have otherwise suffered severe, long-term population decline as a result of habitat loss and fragmentation. Another study showed that birds are generally the first wildlife to visit mine sites following reclamation. Reclaimed mines also provide diverse vegetation that is generally lacking for bird species that rely on early successional habitat. In other words, for some birds, disturbing the soil is actually very helpful, not "devastating."

You don't have to take my word on that. Just ask any birdwatcher from central Illinois who makes regular visits to former surface mines. They want to see birds. And they get to see some unusual ones in surface-mine country. Henslow's sparrows, grasshopper sparrows, savannah sparrows, dickcissels, meadowlarks, indigo buntings, horned larks, upland sandpipers, and loggerhead shrikes are all fairly common in surface mines. They are drawn by the grass and by the opportunity to find nesting areas and prey: small mammals, insects, and seeds.

I'm told we can see all those species and more at Quail Lakes. I've seen several myself and birdwatching friends have seen others. I regularly consult the *Smithsonian Birds of North America* book by Fred Alsop that sits on the coffee table in our cabin. I see birds often and am curious what they are. I saw one the other day that lives on the ground in the prairie grass. It comes up in the grass but never flies out. I'd love to know what that one is. Someday I will. It's pretty enjoyable to spot birds that you don't see anywhere else and then try to guess what they are.

Diane has a sidearm at the ready in case this snake decides to get frisky.

What makes all this even more satisfying is to think that there are so many other species that benefit from grasslands and wetlands that we never see. Studies show reclaimed surface mines also provide habitat

Don Welch, Jerry Foley and I (from left to right) are happy to hold up wild bobwhite quail after a hunt in the prairie grass that surrounds Big Lake.

for several small mammals, amphibians, and reptiles. One fascinating study completed by Michael J. Lannoo and other researchers was completed at Hillenbrand State Fish and Wildlife Area in south central Indiana's Greene County. The site had been surface mined for coal from 1976 to 1982, roughly the same time frame as Quail Lakes. As this was post-law mining, the land was reclaimed according to original contours. Since 1999, the Indiana DNR has been planting native prairie grasses and forbs in scattered blocks. In essence this is a very similar approach to what we have done at Quail Lakes, though we included more row crops in our property than at Hillenbrand.

Findings were fascinating. Researchers discovered 13 species of amphibians (nine frog and four salamander species), including bullfrogs, various tree frogs, leopard frogs, and crawfish frogs. They also documented 19 species of reptiles (one lizard, five turtle, and 13 snake species), including the common kingsnake, North American black racer, yellow-bellied kingsnake, and eastern hog-nosed snake. The list also included two state-endangered species and three species of special con-

Doug Oberhelman

This trio of male wild turkeys was just across the road from Quail Lakes. We have seen increasing numbers of turkeys on the property in recent years.

cern. Amphibian diversity at the study site was comparable to that of a nearby, large restored prairie. That's significant, because amphibians are among the most threatened vertebrate groups on the planet, with one in three species either threatened or extinct.

Lannoo and the other researchers concluded:

> While the act of surface mining coal can reduce and perhaps eliminate populations of amphibians and reptiles, reclamation projects can provide habitat that supports species, including threatened and endangered species. Mine spoil prairies in the southeastern corner of the Illinois Basin provide habitat for a surprising number of amphibian and reptile species, including two state endangered species.
>
> We conclude that mine spoil prairie reclamations can support roughly the same degree of amphibian richness as native prairie restorations, and suggest that planning and permitting decisions for final reclamation and post-mine land use by coal operators, regulatory agencies, and state and federal fish and wildlife agencies take into account the considerable conservation value of these prairie habitats.

While I am not a snake or frog expert, we regularly see both species on our property. It seems safe to assume that many of the other creatures documented in this Indiana study are also crawling around the grassy acres of Quail Lakes. That's a bit creepy and encouraging at the same

Cleaning doves is a common fall ritual at Quail Lakes. I'm joined in this photo by (left to right) Don Welch, Chris Curfman, Joe Colgan, and Rex Linder.

time. I like most wildlife, but not snakes. Diane, on the other hand, doesn't mind snakes. She catches them all the time and we've got pictures of her handling them.

This brings us to another of our favorite stories: "Dicky and The Snake of Big Lake." We kept a jon boat down at Big Lake and the spot where we always flipped it over turned out to be a snake den or something. One day my lawyer and good friend Dick Laukitis came out to Quail Lakes to go fishing. He had been showing off his rowing skills while fishing when, all of the sudden, a big snake popped up from below a seat. This happened right in the middle of Big Lake. He finally managed to get the snake out of the boat, but only after punching a hole through the aluminum floor. Dick barely made it back to shore before the boat sank. Believe me, retelling that story never gets old.

Mammals also respond well to surface mines. Start with the toothy rodents. Muskrats and beavers are fairly common at Quail Lakes. Too common, sometimes. We had a gorgeous maple tree growing at our Cabin Lake, right next to our cabin. We had planted that tree, watered it

Doug Oberhelman

during dry summers and raised it in the hopes it would one day provide plenty of shade. One morning we came out to discover a beaver had cut it down. Big mistake. With the help of a trapper, Diane got the best of that beaver — whose mounted body is now prominently displayed in our cabin.

Another beaver cut down many of the trees in our Wood Duck Hole, the lake I created by damming a ravine in the northeastern portion of Quail Lakes. Muskrats create problems by blocking drainage tubes and undermining dams. Another water-loving mammal has also been a common resident in many surface-mine properties, though they've not yet shown up at Quail Lakes. River otters were reintroduced throughout Illinois in the past three decades and have since been removed from the state threatened and endangered species lists. Surface-mine lakes are one of the many places they now inhabit, including our property at Middle Grove. That's pretty impressive, since for generations nobody saw them at all in central Illinois.

More common sightings include whitetail deer, which bed throughout the grass plantings and around The Big Lake. We've also had a big buck living in the Lower Wetlands the past few years and another trophy buck nearly bowled Allen and me over one day while we were quail hunting. Raccoons and skunks are fairly common, too common actually, as they are deadly predators of ground-nesting birds. We often hear coyotes howling just across the road from us and the other day I chased a young pup down past Big Lake. Squirrels are abundant. I've seen a mink on the property. And we often encounter mice, voles, and shrews. No question, the small mammals respond well to hundreds of acres of grass located right alongside grain fields.

As a hunter, it has also been gratifying to see the comeback of bobwhite quail and even — on a few occasions — pheasants. The species we see out there that I am most partial to are the quail. We've seen coveys throughout the property. In fact, co-author Jeff Lampe, hunting buddies Don Welch and Jerry Foley and I spent one memorable morning flushing wild quail at three different spots on the property. In one grassy area all we found were droppings the quail had left while huddled together for warmth in a circular covey the night before. The last covey was located just south of The Big Lake in prairie grasses we planted 10 years earlier. I can still remember coming around the southwest corner of the lake to see Jeff's Llewellin setter Hawkeye standing still alongside the grass. The sun was perfect, the sky clear and Hawkeye offered up and held the perfect point.

We usually have anywhere from three to five coveys on the property but in 2012, I saw many more than that. We are hoping that continued habitat work will help the bobwhites make a real comeback, because I love seeing them. That was the first gamebird I hunted as a kid in Kansas, where we lived for a few years. We have also had pheasants on the property one year, but they have not yet been able to gain a foothold. I'm hoping that someday pheasants will be more plentiful at Quail Lakes.

The most common gamebirds we see are doves, which roost all over the property and really show up in big numbers in August and September when our sunflower fields mature and drop their seeds. We've had some memorable dove hunts at Quail Lakes, which provides the exact mix that doves seem to love: water, bare ground, grit, old roost trees, and food.

We also regularly see wild turkeys along a creek in the northeast corner. They roost in the big oaks and hickories in that timber which was never mined. They tend to frustrate Diane and me greatly, as we have not had much success hunting them. Even so, that accounts for all four species of the Big Four of forest wildlife that were around when Avery Dalton was toting a shotgun on the property: deer, turkeys, squirrels, and raccoons. We've also got plenty of rabbits roaming the property. It is truly a hunter's paradise. That's something worth noting, as the same is not true for every county in central Illinois.

Nate Herman holds a golden rainbow trout caught by Dave Lampe, my co-author Jeff Lampe's father. Dave had never been ice fishing but caught this rare trout after just a few minutes at Cabin Lake.

Doug Oberhelman

"You look around here at any county that doesn't have strip-mine ground and there's basically very little hunting in it, except around streams and rivers," emphasized veteran wildlife biologist Emerick.

The same can be said for fishing. Sure there are farm ponds and creeks and rivers. But much of the best lake fishing in Illinois is done at surface-mine lakes. That's been true throughout the history of mining in Illinois. As final-cut lakes were created and filled, anglers or mine operators stocked fish in the waters for employees and others to enjoy. Largemouth bass, crappie, bluegill, redear, and channel catfish were the most common species stocked. But that's not all an angler might find in the clear waters of a former mine pit. Some lakes were also stocked with smallmouth bass, some with spotted bass, still others with northern pike, muskie, and bullheads. While most mines allowed public fishing, access was not always easy. As a result, stocked fish had a good chance to grow and multiply.

Over time, anglers began to associate clusters of former surface mines with prime fishing. No wonder then that so many of the Illinois record fish compiled by the IDNR have come from lakes created by mining. That includes all three of the black bass records: Ed Walbel's 13-pound, 1-ounce largemouth bass; Mark Samp's 6-pound, 7-ounce smallmouth bass, and Rick Leonard's record spotted bass of 7 pounds, 3.12 ounces. All three of those record bass came out of deep, steep-sided former mine sites. Walbel caught his lunker largemouth out of a Lake County gravel pit. Samp and Leonard both hooked their fish in former coal mines in Fulton County. All three lakes had fairly limited access. Walbel, for instance, had almost sole fishing rights to the 100-acre quarry that yielded his record, which measured 28 inches and had a girth of 23 inches. Samp was fishing a lake near Farmington on ground once leased by the Spoon River Valley Sportsman Club.

Those are just some of the records. Justin White's record black bullhead of 5 pounds, 6 ounces came out of a Fulton County surface mine on April 24, 1988. Walter Klenzak's 26-pound, 15-ounce record northern pike grew long and strong in a Kankakee County mine lake. Those record fish are an impressive testament to surface-mined lakes.

So is the backing of Ken Russell, a fisheries biologist with the IDNR who since the summer of 1962 has worked with surface mines in Knox, Fulton, Stark, Peoria, and Henry counties. Russell has never been afraid to voice his opinion in favor of surface mines. "I'm a strip-mine advocate," Russell will tell anyone who asks. One such example came in the 1970s when he was invited to speak at the Illinois Audubon Society's annual meeting in Galesburg, Illinois. At first Russell was confused. Why would a fish biologist be invited to speak at a meeting for birdwatchers? "They said, 'We want your slant on surface mining of coal in Illinois,'" Russell recalled. "I told them they might not want to hear what I had to say, but that I would give it to them." And he did.

"I basically said that there are bad things about strip mining and that we've had issues all over the United States with the acid produced from the coal. But here in Illinois, especially in western Illinois, strip mining has been one of the biggest boons to fish and wildlife habitat. You are talking some good standing crops of fish that can be produced in these lakes. They can and do produce excellent sport fisheries. A lot of the people were astonished at what I said and how I backed up with data that [surface mining] was a pretty good thing for fish and wildlife."

Diane's parents Fred and Tilley Allen also enjoy visiting Quail Lakes. Here Sadie admires a largemouth bass Fred caught out of Cabin Lake.

Obviously, not every lake is created equal. Some mine lakes are more fertile than others and produce more fish. Some deep, clear, and less fertile lakes have much less carrying capacity for fish. But from his earliest days of counting and weighing fish in surface-mine lakes, Russell found that the amount of fish produced generally surpassed what experts first expected — including the opinions stated in the go-to source for fisheries managers, George W. Bennett's 1962 book *Management of Artificial Lakes and Ponds*. One year at a conference,

Doug Oberhelman

while presenting this information, Russell was confronted by an unhappy member of the audience — George Bennett. "That was a tough one for me. He was one of my idols almost and he was arguing that my research was wrong," Russell recalled.

But the research was not wrong. The common perception was wrong. That's a big difference we will see again in the next chapter. Our own lakes back up Russell's finding by providing fantastic fishing. And each lake is very different. Northwest Lake has real good fishing like the rest of them. It's primarily a bass and bluegill lake that also produces some nice crappie. Frog Pond is little more than a weedy pond for frogs. Crappie Lake is aptly named because it has some real big crappie and bluegill and a few big bass. Probably the two best fishing lakes are the final-cut lakes on the southeast side of the property.

Cabin Lake is a steep-sided lake with depths up to 65 feet. In addition to huge bluegill, this lake has decent bass, large channel catfish, and an amazing population of rainbow trout that were stocked in October of 2008. Stocking the trout was experimental and was proposed by Nate Herman of Herman Brothers Pond Management in Peoria. When we released 100 rainbow trout that ranged between 6-8 inches, we had no idea for sure what would happen. At first we feared the worst, as the often-finicky trout disappeared by the next summer. But they didn't die — they just went deep. Nate and his brother Justin were able to catch trout by fishing in 30 feet of water — a depth where the trout were able to find water cool enough to survive.

Diane's daughter Alison Cullinan holds up a dove she cleaned at Quail Lakes.

"We were afraid they were gone. But we found out they were living below the thermocline in August. We found them 30 feet deep. We were high-fiving each other when we caught those fish," Nate Herman recalled with a broad smile. "That was really cool." Since then fish from our original stocking have grown to more than four pounds and we have continued to stock more trout, as well as hybrid striped bass.

Big Lake is also steep-sided and has depths of up to 65 feet in its 20 acres. This is a great spot to catch plenty of bass 14-16 inches long, big bluegill, and big crappie. We added a wetland to the northwest corner of the lake that has helped provide food for fish and excellent hunting for ducks and geese. "The water quality in surface-mine lakes is by far better than in a farm pond. The only limiting factor in most surface-mine lakes is food for the fish, because many of them are too infertile to grow lots of fish," Herman emphasized. "By putting in a wetland next to the lake you add bullfrogs and crayfish and minnows and lots of other food that might not be there in a steep-sided surface-mine lake." Big Lake is also the place where we have our goose-hunting pit on the cover. We've had a lot of very good times at that lake.

Dove hunting at Quail Lakes is fun for the women, too. Pictured from left to right are Maureen Cullinan Bennett, Tyson Brill (in background), Kathleen Cullinan Brill, Tilley Allen, and Crystal Curfman.

Given all the benefits to wildlife and the benefits to us as hunters, anglers, birdwatchers and conservationists, it's no wonder attitudes toward surface-mined property have changed. As we shall see in the next chapter, property that was mined for coal has gone from being ignored to pursued in just the last 25 years.

Doug Oberhelman

CHAPTER SIX

FROM WASTELAND TO WONDERLAND

Knox County plat books of the 1960s and 1970s succinctly captured what was once a common opinion of Illinois land that had been surface mined for coal. According to former Midland Coal official Jim Grimm, page after page of the plat books included mine property listed as "Wasteland." It was a harsh judgment that seemed eerily familiar. Remember how the prairie had been seen as a wasteland prior to settlement? Remember how people of the 1700s and the early 1800s mistakenly believed vast grasslands had little worth?

It took time, new technology like John Deere's plow, and a better understanding of the land for early settlers to unlock the vast potential of those prairies. Similarly, Quail Lakes is one of many great examples of how the perception of surface-mine ground eventually changed. Not immediately, though. Until the 1990s the "Wasteland" party line persisted. Once the coal was gone, many figured the only thing that mined property was good for was pasturing livestock. Rocky soil in sites mined before reclamation laws paled in comparison to the black gold soil to which farmers in central Illinois had grown accustomed. Listen to the terms those farmers used to describe surface-mined ground: rough ground, scrub ground, moonscape, and worthless.

Thinking of that today amazes me. Some of my best memories in recent years have come from the "Wasteland" that is Quail Lakes. Diane and I have shared so many great rides, hikes, and hunts out there during our vacations and on the weekends. So have her children, as when her daughter Alison helped dress doves after a hunt or when Maureen and Kathleen learned to shoot their mother's 20-gauge shotgun as teenagers. One of the most vivid memories — which I've mentioned already — is the day we went teal hunting with Diane's son Allen and he became our retriever, wading after downed birds in his bare feet. That was in the Lower Wetlands, an area that was once open 75 feet and probably did look like a wasteland for some time. The point is that description was only accurate in the short-term. But for years that was what many peo-

Here's one of many fine hunts I've enjoyed with Diane's children, in this case Kathleen and Allen.

ple perceived as the legacy of surface-mine property.

Mike Kepple of Peoria heard all that and more when, in 1992, he decided to buy a 1,000-acre piece of mine ground in Fulton County for $450 an acre. His wife Linda was not pleased with the acquisition of Double Cluck Farms, nor was she pleased when he bought another 293 acres of mined ground that same year. "She told me I had lost my mind. She said, 'You are an absolute idiot.' My dad [Ercel Kepple], an old farmer, he thought I was nuts. He thought I was crazy. I think most people thought I was crazy," Kepple recalled with a chuckle. But Kepple had grown up with a shotgun in easy reach and wanted someplace to hunt. He figured surface-mine ground was his cheapest option. "There was never any real plan to make money. I bought it so I could hunt geese. On the business side, I don't know if it ever made sense."

That's not entirely true. In the late 1990s, views began changing about surface-mined ground. As disposable incomes increased, more people invested in former coal mines for recreation. Word of bargains spread. When the calendar flipped to 2000, mine ground in central Illinois had become desirable. Prices soared. In the 1980s and early 1990s selling prices ranged from $300 to $450 per acre. Then price tags increased, quickly moving past $1,000 per acre. Then $1,500. Then $2,000. Within a few years, those who had made "foolish" investments of $450 an acre looked like geniuses. The doom and gloom talk of

Mike Kepple and I (as well as his dog Red) were all smiles during a fall dove hunt at Quail Lakes. Kepple has also worked hard to restore his surface-mine properties.

worthless property stopped. Demand for surface-mined land went through the roof.

"I heard all those stories about the ground will never be the same and will never be worth anything and they are ruining the neighborhood," recalled my friend and property manager Bill Atwood. "Well my God, you can't find any of this [surface-mine] ground that's available now for very long. And look at all the fine lakes we've got. And all the hunting."

Today auctions of surface-mine properties attract large crowds and per-acre prices generally average $2,500 to $3,500. In June of 2012, a sale of 1,460 acres of former surface-mine ground near Canton, Illinois fetched $4.1 million at an auction that drew 140 attendees. The land was mostly reclaimed, though there was one tract of virgin black dirt that brought $8,375 per acre and some rocky pre-reclamation patches that

Doug Oberhelman

brought much less. Overall the property averaged $2,800 per acre — at a time when pundits were still talking about national economic woes. Some at the auction said they believe prices will only get better as the economy improves. For instance, Mike Hitchcock of Canton told the *Peoria Journal Star* he bought a 370-acre parcel at $2,300 per acre as an investment.

That's not unusual according to banker Harold Jehle, who has worked for 43 years at Farmers State Bank in Elmwood, where he is an executive vice president. "To me, recreational ground today is looked at a lot more favorably from the banking side of it, from the standpoint it is an investment," Jehle noted. "The value is going to fluctuate up and down some, but strip-mine ground and your recreational ground has held its own a heckuva lot better than housing."

That view of mine ground as an investment is a relatively new phenomenon. For a long time farmers, realtors and bankers looked at any purchases of mine property with raised eyebrows. Jehle has first-hand knowledge of that. In 1987 he bought 140 acres of surface-mined land south of Elmwood (three miles east of Quail Lakes) for $400 an acre from Midland Coal Company. When the deal was done he heard numerous comments from other landowners in the area, including the late Peoria businessman Dick Whitney. "I'll never forget this. We were at Farm Bureau Park and Dick Whitney said to me, 'What are you doing paying $400 an acre for strip-mine ground,'" Jehle recalled. "I told Dick I didn't buy this for an investment. Mine was a dream."

Jehle grew up in east-central Illinois near Cullom, attended the University of Illinois and worked for the Farm Credit system prior to moving to Elmwood in 1969. In Elmwood he raised a family, built a career and at age 43 fulfilled his dream of buying a lake after years of looking. Natural lakes are rare in Illinois and building man-made lakes is expensive. But surface mines created thousands of lakes, water that is not available everywhere in Illinois. "My tenant over east, he'd kill to have a piece of property like I have," Jehle said of the man who farms his land near Cullom. The problem is there are few lakes in that area — let alone hundreds of all sizes and depths.

Jehle feels he was fortunate to be in the right place at the right time. "Fortunately for me, [by 1987] the mines hadn't recognized that selling this ground as recreational property was a gold mine. All [the mine company] wanted to do was to sell it out at $100 an acre for pasture and in large tracts, 300 to 400 to 500 acres. For me it couldn't have worked out better."

Jehle wound up buying Lake Harold, the name he gave to his 20-acre body of clear, deep water in Elmwood Township. The lake is stocked with numerous species of fish, including largemouth bass, Jehle's favorite. As he approaches retirement, Jehle spends more and more time at the lake. So do his grandchildren, six of whom live near Elmwood. Dove and goose hunting has become a popular pursuit for several of his grandsons. The grandkids also enjoy fishing, camping, and simply spending time outdoors. "And the two grandkids who live in Chicago still come down and want to go out there and use the water, run the four-wheeler and run the jet ski. After my family and the fact I've got good health, [buying the lake] was the best thing that ever happened to me. That's by far one of my best accomplishments, the dream that I was able to fulfill."

Hearing that you can understand why there are no longer any questions about Jehle's decision. In the same vein, at the Kepple household nobody calls Mike crazy any longer — at least not in regard to his purchases of mine ground. "The best investment we've made is in strip-mine ground," Kepple explained. "Those have been my best investments. And we own six companies. I have to remind my wife of this every so often. I say, 'Honey, if you want to look at our financial statement, what's the assets that have meat to them?' It's the farms. And it's because we bought them at such a low price, they've appreciated to such a great value and we've had them long enough to get the mortgages down to almost nothing. So the net worth is tremendous."

Kepple's 1,000-acre Double Cluck Farms has been on the market for $12 million. Yes, that includes outbuildings and a cabin and several wetlands. But it doesn't take an accountant to recognize that $12,000 per acre is a far cry from $450 per acre. "I'll tell you how it unfolded. It was pretty gradual at first. I'd say it started in the late 1990s. It was guys that wanted a place to hunt and fish. Everybody kind of bought their own property to hunt and fish and then the value started going up," Kepple stated. "Deer hunting became popular and the woods got valuable. Goose hunting became a big deal when they started leasing the pits in Fulton County and geese started congregating on Duck Creek

Doug Oberhelman

Power Plant. And it kind of progressed from there. As deer hunting came around and turkey hunting came around and bowhunting got big, industries came about. Fishing. Pro fishing. Outfitters. All that supported the value of the land."

Jehle agreed the increased value of mine ground is a fairly recent development. "Twenty-five years ago, there wasn't much recreational ground. Until the mines started breaking stuff up, there really wasn't such a thing as, 'I want to go out and buy some recreational ground.' What has evolved is that recreation is the name of the game. A lot of people have their disposable money and they want to use it for recreation or to go to Mexico every year." As a result, prices for surface mines have increased steadily since the 1990s. "For me it couldn't have worked out better," Jehle said, smiling.

Landowners across central Illinois who happened to purchase mine property at that time tell similar stories. But the change in views didn't happen overnight. The notion that surface-mined land was worthless persisted for some time after mining stopped. Not so much on reclaimed ground, since that land could once again produce crops. Reclaimed ground pencils out much easier for bankers and landowners. But it was the old mine ground, the rocky, saw-tooth stuff that money counters and tax collectors didn't value. Even Midland Coal officials were not particularly enamored of their property once the coal was gone. "We used to have a vice president [of ASARCO] who looked at all the property as a liability," Phil Christy remembered. "He was a business manager in charge of selling land. He was from New Jersey and didn't know a whole lot about whether it was a soybean or an opossum. He was an accountant."

No doubt Midland officials wondered what they were going to do with 150,000 acres they had accumulated in Peoria, Knox, and Fulton counties. What accountants failed to account for was the wildlife. All those ducks and deer and bass and birds mattered to people. "I remember a businessman coming in to talk to Phil and me and he wanted to buy some pre-law ground [land mined before the 1977 SMRCA Act] that had a lake and some pasture on it. And he said, 'I've put the dollars to this as to how much my cattle can graze and what I can get for it. I can't make it come out to what you guys are asking,' " Grimm recalled. "I remember telling him, 'You are competing against someone that wants

Quail Lakes & Coal

I really enjoy hunting doves in our sunflower fields.

recreational ground. They don't look at it the same way. It's a place for them to hunt and fish. They don't look at rate of return.'"

Even so, Grimm was amazed at how quickly the mine ground sold. Remember, this was supposed to be a wasteland. This was damaged goods. Yet people sought it out. So while Midland Coal's old surface-mine land once sold for as little as $300 an acre in the 1980s when sales started, the final pieces sold in 2012 topped out at $5,400 per acre for cropland and $4,000 for recreational ground. Much of the demand has been driven by hunters and anglers — people like myself and like Kepple who are searching for a place to relax and recreate.

While Kepple would love to say he had a magic ball that told him to buy the 1,000-acre parcel he calls Double Cluck Farm, that's just not true. "Goose hunting was just starting in the area and it was a good goose property right next to Lakeland Park [in Canton, Illinois]," Kepple explained. "I made it tillable to try to get some additional income off of it. It's like everything else in life, being at the right spot at the right time and being lucky. And in my case I happened to buy it because I knew it was there and it was a reasonable price."

Born in 1949, Kepple grew up the youngest of seven children on a dairy farm located between Farmington and Fairview in the heart of Fulton County's surface-mining territory. He came of age at a time when mines were everywhere in that part of central Illinois. "Fulton County was the biggest strip-mine county in the state at that time," he said. For youngsters, there were fringe benefits. Kepple remembers several clandestine fishing trips into the Middle Grove property he eventually bought. "We'd just sneak in the back way."

On many mines there was no need to sneak or slip under fences. Most mine companies didn't care if people fished or swam in the lakes they created, according to Kepple. "Basically you could just come and go. There were some guys that didn't want you on the property, but you had a good feel for where you could and couldn't go. But it was nothing like today. Today you can't go anywhere. Back then, you wanted to go fishing, it was, 'Let's go.' But back then deer hunting was not a deal. Turkey hunting was not a deal. And goose hunting was not a deal. It was fishing, trapping, and some duck hunting."

Swimming was also popular, particularly in lakes that had been mined with a shovel. One common characteristic of those final-cut lakes is that they have a gently tapering slope at one end to allow the shovel to walk itself out of the pit when mining is finished. Those slopes also served as wonderful beaches, including a popular spot at the mile-long lake Diane and I own in Middle Grove. "That lake, Mile Lake, that was the swimming hole for Farmington kids. People would even come from Peoria," Kepple recalled, shaking his head at the thought of a time long gone. "They made their own beach. People would just show up. Nobody knew anybody else. You just put out your beach towel out and went swimming. Frankly, very few people fished."

That has changed dramatically in the years since. Realtors like John O'Reilly of Illinois Land Company frequently get calls from prospective landowners who are seeking surface-mine ground because of the combination of elements those properties possess. Water, trees, and wildlife habitat are hard to come by in much of central Illinois. Not so in surface-mine country. Noted O'Reilly, "They're seeking out recreational ground and they know that strip mine is some of the best recreational ground there is. Ten to 20 years ago it was kind of looked at as ugly

Dick Laukitis and I enjoy spending time fishing at our lakes, so long as there are no water snakes in the boats.

wasted stuff. But now the pits are full. They're nice lakes that are holding fish. It's kind of up and down, so there's a lot of places where deer can hide. So they're growing bigger deer. People know that stuff. They're not necessarily looking for strip-mine ground specifically, but a lot of times that's the result of what they want. And then they are OK with that. Strip-mine ground is no longer a negative element when they think about what kind of ground they want to buy."

There's another advantage to surface-mined properties. Moving earth costs money. And though Caterpillar equipment helps make earthmoving more efficient, costs are sometimes prohibitive for a landowner looking to create a lake or series of wetlands. Surface-mined properties already offer large, deep lakes without having to build a dam. Some older mine sites also have good numbers of smaller lakes and even some seasonally wet areas. For a realtor like O'Reilly, that's significant: "To reproduce some of the lakes that were put in as strip-mine pits, that cost is astronomical. Some of these strip-mine lakes are as big as 40-60 acres. To reproduce that today you're talking $300,000 to $400,000. I have the perfect property in Knox County. With a 25-foot dam you could build a 65-acre lake. We were doing the engineering and surveying for that and we ballparked it at costing $300,000. And we contemplated doing it because it's that cool of a project and would improve the land that much. That's where strip-mine ground has a leg up because those things are in place."

With that in mind, O'Reilly said he has seen surface-mine ground with no improvements sell for as much as $4,000 an acre. "You get into stuff that's been improved or fixed in some way and I've seen $7,000 to $8,000 per acre."

Kepple has also worked hard on his properties, in particular the 1,000-acre Double Cluck Farm. The property was mined in the 1960s well before the strict reclamation laws that proved so beneficial for Quail Lakes. Most of the property was used for pasture until Kepple and his group of investors took over. "There was no black dirt at all. When I bought that in 1992 it had been in pasture since the 1960s. We went in and disked it all up and put in erosion structures in the gullies to stop it from eroding," Kepple explained. "I think we disked it with an industrial disc six times. And we picked up rocks. It's a job. But we got it tillable. We took a strip mine that people said was worthless and we farmed it with yields improving over the years."

You can't just spread fertilizer, plow, and plant though. Surface mining disrupts soil chemistry in dramatic ways. In the case of Double Cluck, the soil was very alkaline after limestone was churned closer to the surface of the soil. Soil pH often runs to 9.0 instead of the desired 7.0. Before fertilizing, farm managers at Double Cluck often add sulfur to lower pH in the wetlands. In the past Kepple even paid to have solid waste from our neighboring Elmwood Farms LLC dairy shipped to Double Cluck. The animal waste helped neutralize the alkaline limestone and bring the pH into balance. But shipping costs are prohibitive — one more reason we are lucky to have the dairy so close to our Quail Lakes operation. "When you plant corn and put nitrogen on it, you can't just pour all kinds of nitrogen on. If your pH is out of whack that nitrogen is not released to the plant," Kepple stressed. "If you have a pH of 9, you can waste thousands of dollars on nitrogen because it's not doing anything."

To complement the tillable ground at Double Cluck, Kepple enrolled hundreds of acres in federal Conservation Reserve Programs that reward landowners who take highly erodible cropland out of production and plant it to native grasses and forbs instead. Double Cluck also has numerous food plots for wildlife and piles of brush and wood are left on the land to serve as habitat for rabbits, quail and other animals. "We've worked really hard to develop populations of pheasants and quail and we have developed populations," Kepple said. "We've got more baby pheasants running around there."

The hard work paid off in many other ways. Today Double Cluck receives about $200 per acre in cash rent for its 350 tillable acres. Another 100 acres are enrolled in CRP and CP-33 — or Conservation Practice 33, which was introduced in 2004 to improve food and habitat for bobwhite quail and other grassland birds. CP-33 is limited to field edges and requires landowners to plant warm-season native grasses and wildflowers. Thanks to the crops and the federal support Double Cluck pays for itself. The farm also provides wonderful recreational opportunities. The goose hunting is often good and the duck hunting has improved dramatically. "Every year the duck hunting gets better and better," Kepple gushed. "There's a lack of food on the Illinois River. And there's siltation. Ducks are moving west. And they get flooded out, so they go to the cornfields. They get to the cornfields and they see flooded corn. And developed property."

Over the years, Kepple believes more ducks are imprinting on surface-mine ground. He said the birds even seek it out over the traditional flyways along the Illinois River. "You can set up at Double Cluck and at about 2:30 or 3 p.m. you can see them coming from Rice Lake [an Illinois River backwater lake]. It starts with specks in the sky. They will cup up from a mile up. They know where they are going. By the time we're done they will be all over the place, landing in the decoys right next to you while you pick up (other decoys). It's a sight. If you like nature, just to sit and watch those ducks is valuable."

As at our Quail Lakes, wild animals and birds of all sorts abound at Double Cluck. In 2012 Kepple said a pair of swans set up shop, though they did not raise cygnets. "We have everything out there. What do you want to see? River otters. Coons. Possums. Skunks. Weasels. Bobcat. And the fishing is fantastic. We took one lake at Double Cluck and made it a smallmouth lake. Only smallmouth bass. You can do anything you want with those lakes. You really can if you take the time and make the investment."

In a landscape dominated by corn and soybeans, that's a desirable attribute for folks who enjoy the outdoors. "As recreational spots get harder and harder to find, there's going to be a day where if you don't own your own property you're not going to fish or hunt," Kepple warned. "Unfortunately, that's the case. And people are putting a premium on recreation. Guys work their butts off all day and they want to go recreate on the weekend. Farmers are leasing ground to outfitters. I don't think it's going to go away." I agree with that. Quail Lakes is just 15 minutes from our home and 30 minutes from my office. Without getting on planes or waiting in an airport we are able to take a leisurely drive to a relatively remote setting that offers lots of things to do.

Kepple has seen more people from urban settings turn to surface-mine country to live or at least to have a weekend home. In his case, he considered purchasing a lake house in northern Wisconsin back in 1992. There were issues with the septic system, so he decided to look closer to Peoria. That's when he opted for the 293-acre parcel at Middle Grove, where he remodeled an old concrete-block building into a weekend retreat. Instead of facing an eight-hour drive to Wisconsin for a weekend at the lake, he drives 40 minutes to Middle Grove. That's an extra half-day of relaxation ... in what somebody once called a wasteland.

O'Reilly concurred. "I don't deal with anyone who wants to go to Wisconsin. People are so busy they want to stay local. Eighty percent of my clients are from Peoria and they want to be within an hour of home. And they are willing to pay extra if it's a half hour."

That has been an issue for taxing bodies in counties that saw significant surface mining, because every step of the process has had tax consequences. In the case of Midland Coal, Grimm said, "The mines never sold their land, because until it was sold [the value and tax rate] stayed what it was prior to mining. That was to keep peace with the townships and the counties. They were paying as though it had never been mined." But after numerous battles with officials in Knox County over permits, Midland decided to sell its ground there. This, you may recall, is the county where the plat book labeled surface mines as "Wasteland." And this is the county where the tax rate for that ground was as low as 25 cents per acre.

I really believe coal should be part of the energy solution for the United States and for the world. But we have to find a way to use it that balances legitimate concerns about our environment with the demands of a world that has a growing population. Photo courtesy of David Zalaznik/Peoria Journal Star.

As mine ground sold and continued to fetch better and better prices, the taxmen caught on. Knox, Peoria, and Fulton counties have re-assessed former mine properties over the years and now tax recreational ground at a much higher rate. In fact, recreational ground is taxed at a much higher rate than farmland. While that's good news for schools, road commissioners, and government bodies that rely on tax dollars, it can put a bind on prospective landowners or those who purchased mine land anticipating one tax bill and then received a much higher bill down the road.

Despite that, and despite the recent economic downturn in the U.S., surface-mine ground has held its value. Sure, prices have dipped some. Folks looking to make big bucks on investments might have been disappointed. But recreational ground has stayed afloat better than the housing market. And long-term, the future looks bright. "I think the value of strip-mine ground is going to continue simply because of recreation. If you look at the Elmwood, Yates City, Farmington area, what's happened

Doug Oberhelman

is people live there. People bought strip mines, built homes, and they live there. It's a lifestyle. Or they built second homes to get out of the city and go recreate," Kepple predicted. "I don't think that value is going to go away."

I completely agree with Mike's logic. And I share his passion for owning land that was once a coal mine. Diane and I bought our property as a getaway place. We didn't get into it planning to do a lot of land restoration. We wanted somewhere to hunt, to fish, and to relax on the weekends and during our vacations. I can drive out there three times a day and not get bored with the drive. It's the sense of arriving someplace where there's nobody around, there's virtually not a telephone pole or anything on that property, and it's ours. And it has everything. It has great fishing and great hunting. It pays for itself with the tillable ground. The whole thing is just very rewarding for me. Home is nice and our other property is nice, but this is the place where we can just kick back and really relax. This is "Ahhhhh!"

The question is, will more mine ground be created in the future? Is there a chance for more surface-mine getaways to be built in the years to come?

The former Midland Coal officials Grimm and Christy don't think so. "I don't ever see coal mining coming back in this area at all ... surface mining in general," Christy predicted. "None of the big companies are running them and there are probably only two or three surface mines in southern Illinois."

They cite the ill feelings of many in the agricultural community of central Illinois as a major impediment to mining. "Towards the end [of his mine work], nobody wanted to sell their land, they wanted to trade it for tax purposes," Grimm recalled. "Our final deal at the Rapatee mine was three acres for one and they wanted pretty much the same soil types."

Then too, permitting under the new reclamation laws created headaches for mine operators. "I don't personally see it coming back," Grimm said. "I think there's too much permitting. And people had a bad taste."

That is unfortunate. Coal needs to be part of our country's energy solution. In the next chapter I will outline why.

CHAPTER SEVEN

THE COAL SOLUTION

So where do we go from here? I really believe coal should be and can be part of the energy solution for the United States and for the world. To some coal is a "dirty" word. But the inconvenient truth is that coal is abundant and relatively cheap and there are ways to make it cleaner to use. Today coal generates between one-third to one-half the electricity consumed in the U.S. and more than 40 percent of the world's electricity. And the cost of coal is competitive compared to natural gas, oil, solar or wind power. A report by the Rand Corporation concluded that market penetration for renewable energy has been limited "primarily by their higher cost relative to fossil energy." But coal gets a bad rap and it is often dismissed when talk turns to the quest for cleaner, more affordable sources of energy. That's a mistake.

Understand we're not looking to return to the days of Avery Dalton, with archaic mining practices and soot darkening the skies. There's no need to go back in time. Cleaner ways to use coal are a real possibility even for developing economies. Instead of turning our back on coal, we must drive technological development that will help us use this resource in a way that reduces emissions and gives the United States a pathway to becoming more energy independent. Coal is a critical piece of our energy puzzle, and we have to find a way to use it that balances the legitimate concerns about our environment with the demands of a world that has a growing population and a growing middle class.

We also have to make coal work in conjunction with wildlife conservation. As the story of Quail Lakes has shown, there are tremendous opportunities to create wildlife habitat in areas that have been mined for coal. As a waterfowl hunter I'm thrilled to see giant Canada geese flying over our property and to know that surface-mined properties helped this species make an amazing comeback from near-extinction. That's one, small successful anecdote. The challenge is to make something similar happen on a larger scale, facing larger environmental concerns. One of my jobs as CEO at Caterpillar is to make sure our company is part of the solution when it comes to issues like these. That's why I'm proud to note that Caterpillar has long been committed to technologies and policies that reduce emissions of all kinds, including greenhouse gases.

Some will say there is no such thing as "cleaner coal." For them, no amount of scrubbing will be enough. They want a world where we don't burn any hydrocarbons. That would be a great world to live in, but it's not realistic anytime soon. There are harsh realities to our existence. We require energy, all of us. Electricity powers the computers that angry activists use, while sitting in air-conditioned rooms, to send email blasts warning of proposed surface mines and other environmental issues. Generating the electricity we often take for granted requires tradeoffs.

I don't think any responsible company has management that says, "We're going to defile the earth to get the oil and coal out." Most people call themselves environmentalists to some degree. People want a clean planet. They want to recycle. They want to use as little energy as they can. Some of that stems from the first Earth Day on April 22, 1970. I remember that well. I was in high school and it was all about the environment and the Vietnam War. Earth Day marked a big change and is really when this country woke up to environmentalism. You can argue that sometimes we go too far with things.

At the same time, look at how much cleaner our water, air, and soil is today than it was in 1970. Mike Conlin was a fisheries biologist for the Illinois Department of Conservation in the 1970s and remembers an Illinois River that often smelled of sewage and was in places covered in foamy bubbles due to all the phosphates in the water. About the only fish species thriving in the Illinois River were carp and goldfish. In the years since the Clean Water Act was passed in 1972, Conlin has seen remarkable changes in water clarity and fish abundance. The bubbles are gone and sauger, walleye, largemouth bass, catfish, and white bass now thrive in the river. "Twenty years later, even 15 years later, we saw tremendous things happen," Conlin recalled. "Water quality increased tremendously."

Comparable gains in water quality have been seen across the country. A recent University of Southern California study showed that water samples off the coast of California have seen a 100-fold decrease in lead and a 400-fold decrease in copper and cadmium. Researcher Sergio Sanudo-

Bill Atwood drives the tractor as I give a hayrack tour of Quail Lakes to a group of Caterpillar employees. See all that corn in the background? That's all growing on land that was surface mined for coal! Photo courtesy of Ben Bean/Caterpillar Inc.

Wilhelmy and his team said the concentrations of metal offshore of Los Angeles are comparable to what you would find in a remote section of Mexico's Baja Peninsula. That's an amazing turnaround.

We've seen similar benefits from the 1990 Clean Air Act amendments, which built on the 1970 Clean Air Act and 1977 amendments.

Those are tremendous changes. The issue is finding a balance between what we're all willing to pay for energy versus what you can do to preserve the resources we have and the environment we live in. It's quite a conundrum for society. All of us want cleaner energy, but hardly anyone will vote for a higher price to make cleaner energy a reality. And most people want to pay less for energy, not more.

It's the same idea that I've mentioned throughout this book regarding land use. Every society has left a footprint on the land, whether with stone hoes or with huge draglines. And every society has required things of the land. Our society, due in part to its size and sophistication, requires much more than ever before. But I don't see that as reason to panic, because we have a greater understanding of environmental concerns and we have much greater technology that can help our society find new ways to lessen our impact on the earth.

One thing I always remember is that when I came to Caterpillar in 1975 there were about 3.5 billion people on the earth. Probably 1.5 billion of those people had electricity. At that time, people were saying the earth could only sustain another 1 to 2 billion people. There was widespread concern that we were going to have food shortages and energy shortages. Today the world's population is 7 billion and there are probably 3.5 to 4 billion people with reliable power. Worldwide about 40 percent of their electricity is generated by burning coal. And we still have energy resources. We still have food. Doomsday has not arrived, and that is due to the tremendous impact of technology.

I am not suggesting that concerns about a sustainable future for food and energy should be ignored. Just the opposite, we need to figure out better ways to utilize and to take advantage of the resources we have on this planet. And we need to do that in a way that has as little impact as possible on the environment. The challenge for us going forward is how do we make sure that 7 billion people on the planet live like those in developed nations without destroying our planet. The challenge is even greater as we approach a world population of 9 billion by 2050. We've got to make sure people in every nation on the planet have access to the same things in life as our generation and that of our ancestors. The question is always one of economics. How do we use the resources we have and make sure there are resources long into the future?

In our case in the United States, many times we don't hear enough about how to save energy and how to use it more wisely. There's a huge amount of energy being wasted that we should take right off the top. We need to turn to cleaner, more efficient appliances. We need to embrace better sources for home air conditioning and heating. We need to insulate our homes and office buildings as best we can. All of that should be promoted across the board because there are opportunities for more efficient use of energy.

Even something as simple as turning off the lights at night can help. I can remember my Dad harping at me about that when I was a kid. I'm sure he wasn't thinking about the impact of one light bulb on the planet, he was just worried about the light bill. But the effect is exactly the same — a lower cost of energy and less impact on the environment. Why don't we as a society get after this in a big way? As I travel around the world there are many countries where you see very few lights on at night. People can't afford to leave them on. We can and should do a better job at that.

Then we need to get to work on alternative sources of energy: nuclear, solar, wind, hydroelectric, and natural gas. They are part of the solution, but each energy source also comes with inherent tradeoffs. Hydroelectric power is among the cleanest, but you can find plenty of studies showing the negative impacts of dams on stream flows and fish populations. As a result, dam is a bad word in this day and age. Many hail wind power as a "green" source of energy. But as more turbines go up across the country, concerns are raised for migrating birds and other issues. In some cases in the U.S., citizens have protested against wind farms because they did not want their view of the landscape "ruined" by large wind turbines. For decades in the U.S., the nuclear power industry has been plagued by cost overruns and safety concerns. Solar energy has yet to prove cost effective.

Finally, new methods for collecting natural gas have provided a great source of energy for America. But there are fears that fracking — hydraulic fracturing of rock layers to release gases for extraction — may contaminate ground water and create air quality issues. If it seems like there's no easy answer, it's because there isn't. All sources of energy have environmental costs as well as benefits.

Even so, I am excited about what's happening with the discovery of this tremendous resource of shale gas deposits. Finding a way to extract natural gas was an engineering and a technological solution that took years to perfect. In fact, fracking began in the 1960s. Only after years of work by scientists, engineers, and geologists have we found feasible ways to release huge supplies of previously untapped energy to the world, especially to the United States. We already are benefitting from that, as the discovery of another abundant energy source has created industries and brought others like plastics and petrochemicals back to the United States. That's because the gas is a feedstock for those industries and with so much now available, it makes business sense for those industries to locate and to grow in the U.S. And we will continue to benefit from this source of affordable energy. I suspect U.S. greenhouse gases will decline with the increased use of natural gas.

What is the cost? Well, if you go out to a fracking site, you will be surprised at how small the footprint is compared to the energy it generates. To me it seems a responsible way to collect huge supplies of natural gas. I also think the key to avoiding contamination should be by focusing on companies that use the best possible practices for fracking. In short, when it is done the right way, we can have access to an abundant supply of energy with a relatively low risk to the environment. In my opinion, what fracking has already done for this country in terms of lowering our energy costs and reducing our CO_2 emissions is remarkable. It's a great tradeoff. And I really believe most companies involved are responsible. There's no question regulations have made our country and our planet better. But when it gets down to it, those writing regulations and living by regulations generally want to do the right thing.

Our U.S. economy has been built on fairly cheap, abundant energy and continues to rely on that energy. The discovery of new ways to collect natural gas is helping in that regard, and I think burning natural gas can also buy us time until we find a cleaner way to use coal. For one thing, burning natural gas is already reducing CO_2 emissions. Burning natural gas is also reducing the demand for coal. But not forever. At some point, when there is enough demand created to burn natural gas in cars, trucks, bulldozers, and in other ways, prices will go up and coal will look attractive again to companies who generate power.

That reminds me of the old phrase, "You've got to dance with the one that brought you." Coal has played a huge role in building the United States. The story of Quail Lakes is just one of countless illustrations of that role. Coal helped Avery Dalton prosper after he settled in central Illinois. Coal helped the nearby town of Elmwood light its streets and heat its homes.

As I said earlier, coal still has to be part of the American energy solution. It is abundant and relatively cheap to use. Coal offers a stable source of energy that allows us to avoid reliance on energy sources from other countries. What we need to develop are cleaner ways to burn the high-sulfur coal found in states like Illinois. I am absolutely confident we will find a way to get that done through continuing advances in technology.

One example of the innovation I know is possible is in China at the

Quail Lakes & Coal

Seeing bobwhite quail like this at our restored Quail Lakes property is a very gratifying experience.

Sihe Coal Mine in Jincheng City, Shanxi Province. There, at the world's largest methane-run power plant, you will find 60 Caterpillar methane-gas-powered generators that were built at a Caterpillar plant in Lafayette, Indiana. These generators burn methane gas collected from the Sihe Coal Mine. Previously, the methane gas from coal was just flared into the environment. That had an environmental impact and also wasted a potential source of energy. Now the power plant captures methane gas and Cat generators burn that methane to create 120 megawatts of electricity that goes into the power grid. This is a perfect example of the technological advances I'm talking about. And it's particularly significant since China is the world's largest consumer of coal. China deserves the lowest energy cost possible but we also want to balance and find ways to reduce greenhouse gas emissions. It's a massive balancing act, really. We've got to find a way to make that balance affordable.

For several years I was on the board of directors at Ameren Corporation, the nation's fourth-largest user of coal. Some Ameren power plants, because of the quality of the scrubbers in their smokestacks, can burn a mix of coal from the Powder River Basin of Wyoming and from Illinois. Because they burn some coal locally they save on the cost of freight. That's a huge savings, since the cost of coal is roughly equal to the cost of transportation from the Powder River Basin. If you are paying $10 a ton for coal out of the Powder River Basin it costs you $10 more in transportation. If you can figure out how to burn that coal and pay virtually nothing for freight, because you are sitting next to the coal, that's a pretty good deal. That's one reason it is so attractive.

To me burning coal close to home also makes more sense than another option we are seeing today. I watched the southern Illinois mines and many other mines in the country shut down 20 years ago. Yet today, southern Illinois mines have reopened and they are exporting coal to China and India. We freight coal by railroad to the West Coast, then sail it to China, and they burn it there. In short, the high-sulfur coal is still getting burned, even if it is on the other side of the world. That's amazing to me. Until we can figure out how to use coal globally, what's the difference if it is burned in Illinois or China if we are worried about CO 2? That said, one major difference is that you burn a lot more CO 2s transporting coal from the mine in southern Illinois to Asia. Somehow, global leaders must find a way to solve this very difficult dilemma.

Actually, that's true across our country, which is often called the Saudi Arabia of coal. We have more coal reserves than any other country in the world and 28 percent of the world's total coal supply. According to America'sPower.org, the U.S. has 267 billion tons of coal reserves and currently uses 1.1 billion tons of coal per year. That's a good position to be in, as world coal consumption is growing faster than the consumption of any other kind of energy according to the Intergovernmental Panel on Climate Change (IPCC). The IPCC estimated demand for coal by 2030 will be double that of 2007. Here in the United States we rely on coal for about one-third of our energy production and we export about 6 percent of the coal we mine.

Consider this Presidential Memorandum issued by President Obama on February 3, 2010: "For decades, the coal industry has supported quality high-paying jobs for American workers, and coal has provided an important domestic source of reliable, affordable energy. At the same time, coal-fired power plants are the largest contributor to U.S. greenhouse gas emissions and coal accounts for 40 percent of global emissions.

Charting a path toward clean coal is essential to achieving my Administration's goals of providing clean energy, supporting American jobs, and reducing emissions of carbon pollution. Rapid commercial development and deployment of clean coal technologies, particularly carbon capture and storage (CCS), will help position the United States as a leader in the global clean energy race." On that the President and I agree.

The potential is also there for Illinois, which has the largest overall bituminous coal reserves and the largest, strippable bituminous coal reserves in the United States. According to the Illinois State Geological Survey, 211 billion tons of bituminous coal lies under the surface of the state, having a total heating value greater than the estimated oil deposits in the Arabian Peninsula. Yes, there are concerns about the sulfur content in Illinois coal and the resulting sulfur dioxide and mercury emissions. That's one reason the EPA has issued national rules requiring coal-fired power plants to limit airborne mercury emissions and other air pollutants by 2015. Most agree we can meet those limits with the technology already at hand. But there's room for even more technological improvement.

Remember the big debate a few years ago about acid rain, which was caused by sulfur dioxide and nitrogen oxide emissions? Once the problems of acid rain were documented, we found ways to solve the problem. Amendments to the Clean Air Act had required reductions of sulfur dioxide emissions nationwide. One way those objectives were met was by the establishment of a trading exchange program, which reduced sulfur dioxide emissions nationwide. Also, by using catalytic converters, vehicles became cleaner under the EPA's mobile source regulations. Sure enough, we don't hear much about acid rain any longer. That was a technological and engineering solution. The solution for coal going forward will be the same: technology and engineering. Somebody will devise a way that we can use coal in a cleaner, yet still-affordable fashion.

The answer could include carbon sequestration, or better scrubbers or a whole array of other things, some of which have yet to be discovered. The story of acid rain provides a road map of what we can do with technology. Another environmental problem we've had success solving were the chlorofluorocarbons (CFCs). Remember the great hole in the ozone layer that was letting our earth's atmosphere escape? Well, you don't hear much about that any more. Why? In the 1990s we banned aerosol sprays that contained CFCs and began to switch refrigerators and air conditioners away from chemicals that contained CFCs. Since then, several studies have shown that ozone depletion in the upper atmosphere has slowed dramatically in the last decade. That was a solution through engineering and technology.

The solution for using hydrocarbons is ahead of us. We just have to figure it out. Somebody will. That period of time, whether it's five years or 50 years gives engineers a long time to figure out how to burn coal with fewer emissions. I've heard the climate change challenge compared to the space race. In 1961 President John F. Kennedy challenged a generation to develop the technology that put a man on the moon in less than a decade. We need that same energy and drive to motivate a new generation to rise to the challenges presented by growing energy needs and the threats of global warming. If we can work together with a common goal, I have every confidence in our ability to address climate change and create economic opportunity. Everybody in the world wants to find the silver bullet that makes coal a "clean" alternative fuel source. Somebody will.

Overcoming negative attitudes toward coal will not be easy. Much of the coal that can be mined in the United States is in rural areas. In many of those rural communities there is lingering resentment toward mining and the loss of tillable ground, even though modern reclamation laws require cropland be returned to cropland — something that does not happen in the case of housing developments. Soaring prices of tillable ground will also make it harder to acquire large parcels for mining.

But I think the story of Quail Lakes spells out how we can use coal for the good of our society, for the good of wildlife, and for the good of agriculture. There are benefits to coal that go beyond energy, as we've outlined in this book. Mines create jobs, directly and indirectly. Surface-mined properties provide excellent wildlife habitat. Those same properties provide wonderful recreational areas.

So I end up where I began this project, impressed by the role our little central Illinois property has played. Over the years Quail Lakes has provided so much for so many. Wild game. Corn. Beans. Hay. Timber. Wheat. Coal. Electricity. Milk. Wildlife habitat. Recreational opportunities. Yet if you were to visit our property today, you'd never know it was once a surface mine. Amazing!

END NOTES & BIBLIOGRAPHY

I enjoy history, particularly reading about Native Americans. But I am no historian. I'm also not an expert on coal mining or the evolution of land reclamation in Illinois and the United States. Fortunately, there is a wealth of research available on those subjects. In the course of writing this book, Jeff Lampe and I consulted numerous sources. Here is information on those sources.

While tracing the history of native people in Illinois for Chapter 1, we turned often to research by Dickson Mounds Museum and the Illinois State Museum. If you have not visited those fine museums, you are missing out on fascinating accounts of Illinois history. The story of native inhabitants is displayed throughout the museums and online.

To trace the story of Avery Dalton, we read numerous newspaper articles and biographical sketches, including Johnson & Company's 1880 *The History of Peoria County*. That same history book (we referred to several editions) is also a good source for statistics about agriculture, land values, and population in Peoria County. For historical information about Elmwood Township and the land that would become Quail Lakes, *Elmwood 2004* was a helpful source. Another fine source for Elmwood historical information is the Lorado Taft Museum at 302 N. Magnolia St. in Elmwood, home of the Elmwood Historical Society.

There are many versions of the accounts of Pere Jacque Marquette and Louis Jolliet and the other explorers who came to Illinois. There are also many spelling of their names! The Wisconsin Historical Society has a wonderful online archive dedicated to "Eyewitness Accounts of Early American Exploration and Settlement." Those archives include the historic diaries of Marquette and Jolliet.

Dr. James Lewis also assembled a fine source of online information on the Black Hawk War in his *Background: The Black Hawk War of 1832* Abraham Lincoln Digitization Project through Northern Illinois University.

For information about John Deere and John Lane we referred to various sources, including "The Impact of John Deere's Plow," an article by

Doug Oberhelman

Hiram M. Drache published in the *Illinois History Teacher*. For specific numbers about John Deere plow sales we referred to the John Deere company website.

While researching Chapter 2 we found facts and figures for Illinois coal mining primarily from the *Coal Report of Illinois*, published annually by the Illinois Department of Mines and Minerals. We also read through several annual reports and publications regarding coal that were published by the Illinois Department of Commerce and Economic Opportunity.

To trace the history of Peabody Coal Company, we referred to the online history provided by Peabody Energy on its website.

Our historical review of surface mining and coal mining in general also included perusing the second edition of *Surface Mining*, edited by B. A. Kennedy. And James Krohe Jr. wrote and researched an insightful series of articles on coal mining for *Illinois Issues* in 1979, the most relevant of which was called "Corn, coal, corn: strip mining and reclamation."

There's also much good information provided in *Geology of Illinois* by the Illinois State Geological Survey. That reference tome provides information on surface mining, coal-mining statistics, and the history of Illinois coal deposits.

For Chapter 3 we admired page after page of stories and pictures about big shovels, monster draglines, and other earthmoving marvels. The list of books consulted is long and the titles are impressive.

In Chapter 4 while detailing the 1976 Surface Mining Control and Reclamation Act we turned frequently to the *Citizen's Guide to Coal Mining and Reclamation in Illinois* by the Illinois Department of Natural Resources. For quotations from Presidents Ford and Carter, we referred to online presidential libraries.

An obvious source for Chapter 5 was *The Giant Canada Goose*, by Harold C. Hanson, since surface mines have played such an integral part in the comeback of these big birds.

Beyond those are several other sources, which we list here.

BIBLIOGRAPHY

- Alsop, Fred J. *Smithsonian Birds of North America*. New York: DK Publishing. 2001. Print.

• American Journeys. Wisconsin Historical Society. 2011. Web. June, August 2012.

• Beck, Lewis C. *A Gazetteer of the States of Illinois and Missouri.* Albany, New York: Charles R. and George Webster. 1823. Web. July 2012.

• Bennett, George W. *Management of Artificial Lakes and Ponds.* New York: Reinhold Publishing Corp. 1962. Web. June 2012.

• Boggess, Arthur C. *The Settlement of Illinois, 1778-1830.* Chicago: Chicago Historical Society. 1908. Web. July, September 2012.

• Bolt, Martin. *Thirtieth Annual Coal Report of Illinois.* Springfield, Illinois: Illinois State Journal Co. 1912. Web. June, August 2012.

• Brauning, D. W., M. C. Brittingham, D.A. Gross, R.C. Leberman, T.L. Master, and R.S. Mulvihill. "Pennsylvania breeding birds of special concern: A listing rationale and status update." *Journal of Pennsylvania Academy of Science.* 68: 3-28. 1994. Web. June 2012.

• Brauning, D., M. Grishaver, and C. Grainer. "Nesting-season responses of three grassland sparrow species to previous-year mowing on reclaimed surface mines in Clarion County, Pennsylvania." *Journal of Pennsylvania Academy of Science.* 75: 23-26. 2001. Web. June 2012.

• Cady, Gilbert H. *Illinois Coal Mining Investigations.* Urbana, Illinois: Illinois State Geological Survey. 1915. Web. June, July 2012.

• Chandler, Alred D. "Anthracite Coal and the Beginnings of the Industrial Revolution in the United States." *The Business History Review.* 46:2. Web. July 2012.

• Cronon, William. *Changes in the Land – Indians, Colonists, and the Ecology of New England.* New York: Hill & Wang. 1983.

• Dalton, Roscoe. *Memories of a Prairie Boyhood.* Farmington: Hound Empire Press. 1991. Print.

• Davenport, Paula. "SIUC researchers guide return of trumpeter swans." *SIU News.* Feb. 12, 2002. Web. July 2012.

• DeNeal, Brian. "Shawnee National Forest/Peabody Energy land swap received negatively." *Harrisburg Daily Register.* Jan. 25, 2012. Web. May 2012.

• Drache, Hiram M. The Impact of John Deere's Plow. *Illinois History Teacher.* 8:1, 2-13. 2001. Web. June 2012.

• DuBois, Stanley. *Boys of Elmwood,* Self-published. Print.

• Eichholz, Michael W. and Dana M. Varner. "Survival of Wisconsin

Interior Population of Trumpeter Swans." *Southern Illinois University.* Web. July 2012.
- Elmwood Historical Society. *Elmwood 2004*. Batavia, Illinois: Filter Media. 2004. Print.
- Franke, Judith A. *French Peoria and the Illinois Country 1673-1846*. Springfield, Illinois: Illinois State Museum Society. 1995. Print.
- Galligan, E. W., T. L. DeVault, and S. L. Lima. "Nesting success of grassland and savanna birds on reclaimed surface coal mines of the midwestern United States." *Wilson Journal of Ornithology*. 118: 537-546. 2006. Web. June 2012.
- Galloway, Paul. "Blacksmith Forges an Industry on the Illinois Prairie." *Chicago Tribune*. August 31, 1987. Web. July 2012.
- Garland, Hamlin. *Boy Life on the Prairie*. New York: The Macmillan Company. 1899. Web. May 2012.
- Gordon, Hanford Lennox. *Indian Legends and Other Poems*. Salem, Massachusetts: Salem Press Company. 1910. Web. June 2012.
- Guither, Harold D. "Illinois Lands Affected by Strip Mining." *Illinois Agricultural Economics*. 14:2. 1974. Web. May 2012.
- Haddock, Keith. *The Earthmover Encyclopedia*. St. Paul, Minnesota: Motorbooks. 2002. Print.
- -----------. *Colossal Earthmovers*. Osceola, Wisconsin: MBI Publishing Company. 2000. Print.
- -----------. *Giant Earthmovers An Illustrated History*. Osceola, Wisconsin: MBI Publishing Company. 1998. Print.
- Hall, J. Knox (Editor). *History of Stark County*. Chicago: The Pioneer Publishing Company. 1916. Print.
- Hanson, Harold C. *The Giant Canada Goose*. Carbondale, Illinois: Southern Illinois University Press. 1997. Print.
- Havera, Stephen P. *Waterfowl of Illinois*. San Diego, Phoenix Publishing. 1998. Print.
- Haycraft, William R. *Yellow Steel – The Story of the Earthmoving Equipment Industry*. Urbana, Illinois: University of Illinois Press. 2000. Print.
- *The History of Peoria County Illinois*. Chicago, Johnson & Company. 1880 and 1902. Print.
- *The History of Fulton County Illinois*. Peoria, Illinois: Chas. C. Chapman & Co. 1879. Print.

- Hoffmeister, Donald F. *Mammals of Illinois*. Urbana, Illinois: University of Illinois Press. 2002. Print.
- Illinois Department of Mines and Minerals. *Coal Report of Illinois — 1976*. Springfield, Illinois: Illinois Department of Mines and Minerals. 1976. Web. May, June, August 2012.
- Irving, Washington. *A Tour on The Prairies*. Paris: Galignani and Co. 1835. Web. May, August 2012.
- Office of Mines and Minerals. *Citizen's Guide to Coal Mining and Reclamation in Illinois*. Springfield: Illinois Department of Natural Resources. 1993. Web. June, July and August 2012.
- James, Steve. "Coal makes a comeback in Illinois Basin in U.S." *Reuters*. May 11, 2012. Web. June 2012.
- Kennedy, Bruce A. (Editor). *Surface Mining*. Littleton, Colorado: Society for Mining, Metallurgy, and Exploration. 1990. Print.
- Kiner, Henry L. *The History of Henry County, Illinois*. Chicago: The Pioneer Publishing Company. 1910. Web. April 2012.
- Klepper, Michael and Michael Gunther. *The Wealthy 100: From Benjamin Franklin to Bill Gates — A Ranking of the Richest Americans, Past and Present*. Seacaucus, New Jersey: Carol Publishing Group. 1996. Web. July 2012.
- Kolata, D.R., and C.K. Nimz (Editors). *Geology of Illinois*. Illinois State Geological Survey. 2010. Print.
- Krohe, James Jr. "Corn, coal, corn: strip mining and reclamation." *Illinois Issues*. July 1980. Web. June 2012.
- Kulier, Jennifer. "From Wastelands to Wetlands." *Perspectives*. Southern Illinois University Carbondale. Fall 2000. Web. June 2012.
- Ladd, Doug. *Tallgrass Prairie Wildflowers*. Helena, Mont.: Falcon Publishing, Inc. 1995. Print.
- Lannoo, Michael J. et al. "Mine Spoil Prairies Expand Critical Habitat for Endangered and Threatened Amphibian and Reptile Species." *Diversity*. 1:2 2009. Web. July 2012.
- Lewis, James. "Background: The Black Hawk War of 1832." *Abraham Lincoln Digitization Project*. Northern Illinois University. Web. June 2012.
- Leyland, Marilyn J. "A History Underground – Coal Mining in the Peoria Area." *InterBusiness Issues*. April 2012. Web. July 2012.
- Mattice, Jennifer A., Daniel W. Brauning, and Duane R. Diefen-

bach. "Abundance of Grassland Sparrows on Reclaimed Surface Mines in Western Pennsylvania." *USDA Forest Service Gen. Tech. Rep.* 2005. Web. July 2012.

- Merritt, H. Clay. *The Shadow of A Gun*. Chicago: F.T. Peterson Company. 1904. Print.
- Nolde, Gilbert C. (Editor). *All in a Day's Work – Seventy-Five Years of Caterpillar*. Forbes Custom Publishing. 2000. Print.
- Office of Coal Development. *2010 – The Illinois Coal Industry*. Springfield: Department of Commerce and Economic Opportunity. 2010. Web. May, June, July 2012.
- Orlemann, Eric C. *Giant Earth-Moving Equipment*. Osceola, Wisconsin: Motorbooks International. 1995. Print.
- -----------. *Power Shovels: The World's Mightiest Mining and Construction Excavators*. St. Paul, Minnesota: Motorbooks International. 2003. Print.
- -----------. *The Caterpillar Century*. Minneapolis, Minnesota: Motorbooks. 2007. Print.
- *Portrait and Biographical Album of Peoria County, Illinois*. Chicago: Biographical Publishing Co. 1890. Print.
- Prince, Hugh. *Wetlands of the American Midwest*. Chicago: University of Chicago Press. 1997. Print.
- Robertson, Estelle W. *One Hundred Years in the History of Elmwood Illinois*. 1935.
- Rummel, Shawn M. and Fred. J. Brenner. "Use of Grassland Avian Communities to Monitor Reclamation Success on Surface Mine Lands." Gillette, Wyoming: American Society of Mining and Reclamation. 2007. Web. June 2012.
- Shallenberger, Eliza Jane. *Stark County and its Pioneers*. Cambridge, Illinois: B.W. Seaton. 1876. Web. May, June 2012.
- Warren, Robert E. and John A. Walthall. "Illini Indians in the Illinois Country, 1673-1832." . 60(1). Web. July 2012.
- -----------. "Illini archaeology: cultural heritage and repatriation." *The Living Museum*. 60(2). Web. July 2012.
- Wickett, Justin. "Coal in Human History." *Duke University*. 2008. Web. June, July 2012.
- Williamson, Bob. *Giant Canada Goose Restoration and Management in Illinois*. Springfield: Illinois Department of Conservation. Web.

June 2012.
- World Coal Institute. *The Coal Resource: A Comprehensive Overview of Coal*. N.p. n.d. Web. June 2012.
- -----------. *History of Coal Use*. N.p. n.d. Web. June 2012.